Power of Rave

Wisdom of Serp

Power of Raven
Wisdom of Serpent

Celtic Women's Spirituality

Noragh Jones

Floris Books

First published in 1994 by Floris Books
Reprinted in 1995

British Library CIP Data available

ISBN 0-86315-186-8

Printed in Great Britain
by Cromwell Press, Wilts

Contents

Acknowledgments

I would like to thank Wild Goose Publications, the publishing wing of the Iona Community, for permission to quote extracts from the Iona Pilgrimage (pp.60-64 of the *Iona Community Worship Book,* revised edition, 1991). My grateful thanks to Dr Alison Hills (now Neisser) for passing on to me a copy of the ceremony at the opening of her new surgery, which she based on forms from the *Carmina Gadelica.*

I was greatly helped in the preparation of this book by the responses of my extramural classes to material from the *Carmina Gadelica* which I presented in a series of discussions in 1991 and 1992 on "What is Celtic Christianity?" and "Swapping Samplers with the Angels." These classes were held under the auspices of the University of Wales Aberystwyth Extramural Department, to whom I am grateful for their continuing encouragement of my interests in Celtic spirituality.

Foreword

Many people are now turning to the Celtic traditions to help give spiritual guidance and depth of meaning to modern life. Chief among these sources is Alexander Carmichael's *Carmina Gadelica,* a treasury of Gaelic blessings and prayers which are both practical and deeply mystical. First published in 1900, they derive from the crofting folk of the Western Highlands and Islands, who lived by land and sea, in an ancient life-style which had changed little until the last hundred and fifty years.

From raising the fire in the morning to smooring it for the night, from birth to death, from beginning work to its ending, Gaelic men and women wove a continual thread of prayer and blessing. No work was begun without its special prayer, no garment was first put on without a blessing being breathed over its wearer, no journey was attempted without a traveller's invocation for protection. Those who prayed for the day and its work, for the soul and its life, became guardians of the deep spiritual connection between all forms of life, both seen and unseen.

In a world that "boasts" of the nuclear family, self-sufficiency and independence from any spiritual ground, Noragh Jones' book comes as a timely reminder of our true connection to life. Our grandmothers would not have relished our isolating life-style, for they had the humility which is truly rooted in the realities of life. They knew that without family, neighbours, livestock, plants or spiritual support they simply had no belonging to the earth.

It is a shock to realize just how much the reality of urban isolation has now become a yardstick for "normal" existence over much of the globe. Separation from our neighbour, our family, our earth and its living beings — whether furred, feathered, finned or leafed — is almost complete. We are all in danger of becoming forever separated from the deep, spiritual connection that sustained our foremothers and forefathers.

This book particularly traces the contribution of women in helping maintain that connection. It is commonly held that women are natural repositories of lore, custom and belief, an understanding that was sustainable in a culture where women kept the hearth. But is it so today? Swept into the maelstrom of a daily wage-earning existence, where family life and quality time are relegated to a few moments before bedtime, women lose the space in their lives for prayerful reflection and traditional recollection. But it is not too late for women today to resume their power as hearth-keepers who keep the memories strong, who uphold the integrity of love and truth, who keep bright the songs and stories which inspire.

The hearth is the first altar, sacred both to St Brighid as well as to *her* forerunner, the goddess Brighid. Neither is a lady who would tolerate the peevish modern term "housewife," with all its disempowering connotations. A woman can be a hearth-keeper as well as wage-earner, vigorous, able and hospitable: a true keeper of the flame of life itself who rekindles enthusiasm in the discouraged, who strengthens the despairing, who counsels the undecided, who inflames all hearts to act justly and effectively. Noragh Jones' heartfelt plea for the extension of these qualities of the Celtic hearth-keeper to public organizations and governmental policy-making is one which many women echo. Not to be governed from commonly held but hollow dogmas and impractical theories, but from the very heart of life as it is really lived — that is the wish drawn from the experience of women, the hearth-keepers and life-givers.

In what way can these Gaelic prayers and blessings help us now? The crofting culture from which they derive may seem to many as too remote from modern life to provide any helpful guidance. But however and wherever we live in the world, we each follow our soul's path through life, we each experience fear, need and pain. The weaving of blessings and prayers is not relegated to the country-dweller nor to the card-carrying religious person; it is a vibrant and essential duty which upholds our common life, allowing help and inspiration to flow. When stark need strikes us, sharp as hunger or sexual desire, we need no priest to utter the blessing, the words well up from the heart's depth unaided.

Throughout Gaelic prayer, the mantle of Brighid is invoked as a palladium against danger, injury or attack. *Power of Raven, Wisdom of Serpent* reweaves the sacred mantle of blessing and song, placing it lovingly about the shoulders of our desacralized world.

Brighid of the Mantle, encompass us,
Lady of the Lambs, protect us,
Keeper of the Hearth, kindle us,
Beneath your mantle gather us,
And restore us to memory.

Mothers of our mother,
Foremothers strong,
Guide our hands in yours,
Remind us how
To kindle the hearth,
To keep it bright,
To preserve the flame,
Your hands upon ours,
Our hands within yours,
To kindle the light
Both day and night.

The Mantle of Brighid about us,
The memory of Brighid within us,
The protection of Brighid keeping us
From harm, from ignorance, from heartlessness,
This day and night,
From dawn till dark,
From dark till dawn.

Caitlín Matthews
Oxford, Midwinter 1993

Introduction

Many women today are looking for new forms of spirituality which connect with our own everyday lives and speak with our own voices. And many men are becoming more aware of the need for wholeness in our spiritual communities which includes women's experiences and insights as well as men's. But where do we find the models in the Christian tradition to give us a start? This book explores the lives of Gaelic women in the Highlands and Islands of Scotland, who helped to shape that Celtic Christianity which had its roots in the Isle of Iona, where Columba founded his monastery in the sixth century.

These women lived lives of material hardship in the crofting communities which were broken and scattered during the Clearances of the eighteenth and nineteenth centuries, when the land was given over to sheep farming on a large scale, and many of the people went on emigrant ships to Canada and Australia. But their prayers and blessings and old tales were collected a hundred years ago by Alexander Carmichael who became their personal friend and fought to get the Crofters' Commission set up in the 1880s to save what was left of their way of life. They can still teach us human warmth and compassion.

The crofters had no security of tenure till after the shocking revelations of the Royal Commission on Crofting Communities. Incomers (often lowland farmers) took over the crofting land for sheep runs as an "improvement scheme" instigated by the land-owners, and the families were cleared off to marginal land by the seashore or to the emigrant ships. In many cases their own ministers urged them to obey the powers that be and await their reward in heaven. As Catherine MacPhee of Iochdar on the Isle of Uist remembered the Clearances:

Many a thing have I seen in my own day and generation, many a thing, O Mary Mother of the black sorrow! I have

seen the townships swept, and the big holdings being
made out of them, the people being driven out of the
countryside to the streets of Glasgow and to the wilds of
Canada, such of them as did not die of hunger and plague
and smallpox while going across the ocean. I have seen
the women putting the children into the carts that were
sent from Benbecula and the Iochdar to Loch Boisdale,
while their men lay bound in the pen and were weeping
beside them, without power to give them a helping hand,
though the women themselves were crying aloud and
their little children wailing like to break their hearts.
I have seen the big strong men, the champions of the
countryside, the stalwarts of the world, being bound on
Loch Boisdale quay, and cast into the ship as would be
done to a batch of horses or cattle in the boat, the bailiffs
and the ground-officers and the constables and the
policemen gathered behind them, after them ...[1]

Alexander Carmichael spent a lifetime travelling around the
Highlands and Islands in the second half of the nineteenth
century collecting what was left of the old Gaelic lore, both
Christian and pagan. During that time he observed with sadness
and distress the three-pronged attack on the culture that came
from the Clearances, the introduction of more puritanical forms
of Christianity, and the effect of the network of board schools
which used English rather than the Gaelic language of the
people as the basis of education. Catherine MacPhee told him
that in the old days the people had been full of music and song,
of hymns and of prayers.

By the Book itself, you would not ask but to be hearing
them, however long the night, however wild the weather,
however miry the road, however dark the small hours
going home. That was our school and we had no other.
There was but one school in South Uist between the
Stack of Eriskay and the Isle of Floday, nearly forty
miles' journey, with three ferries to make, three sounds to
cross. That was very different from the children of today
— a school at every door.

Peggy MacCormack of Loch Boisdale remembered that while the crofters still held the land:

> The people were strong, healthy and happy and enjoyed
> life to the full in their plain, homely ways. They had
> sheep and cattle, corn, potatoes and poultry, milk, cheese,
> butter and fish, all in sufficiency. They were good to the
> poor, kind to the stranger, and helpful to one another,
> and there was nothing amiss ... But the Clearances came
> upon us, destroying all, turning our small crofts into big
> farms for the stranger, and turning our joy into misery,
> our gladness into bitterness, our blessing into blasphemy,
> and our Christianity into mockery.[2]

Sentimental exaggeration? Hardly, for in one glen in South Uist — Corradale — eighty-two crofter families were evicted, and the whole district was emptied of people, "many of them to die moral and physical deaths in the slums of Glasgow and other cities — in order to add their land to the already extensive lands of tacksmen, one of these being the parish minister," Carmichael notes.

The cultural and spiritual loss was irremediable, as well as the material hardships. For when ministers condemned and strangers were either indifferent or hurtfully derisive about the Gaelic culture, the younger generations soon learned to mock and jeer. Their parents and grandparents developed that half-ashamed self-consciousness that comes when minority cultures are declining and on the defensive. They stopped passing on what they knew from the oral tradition, and left the education of their young in the hands of the school teachers and the ministers (and later the media). The new culture of literacy unfortunately devalued in people's minds and hearts the old oral culture, and little was left of traditional Gaelic Christianity, with its unique blend of sacred and secular, spiritual and practical, personal and universal. When Carmichael was taking down runes and songs from Mary Mackintosh in South Uist towards the end of the century, he observed the differences that had occurred since he had visited her father Patrick Smith forty years before:

His grandsons and granddaughters were full of modern
so-called education, and of self-sufficiency, and of un-
abashed disdain for their unlettered old grandfather and
for his traditional lore. Unasked they showed their own
advancement by singing music hall songs and ditties and
by reciting music hall slang and vulgarities ... The
difference between the quiet simple dignity and repose of
the unlettered old Patrick Smith and his forward, aggressive, talkative grandchildren was grievous as it was
striking. Not less striking was the contrast between the
beautiful and elevated old lore of the old man and the
vulgar modern literature of the young people.[3]

To highlight the contrast, he gives us a good wish which Mary
Mackintosh recited to him on that visit:

> Power of raven be yours,
> Power of eagle be yours,
> Power of the Fiann.
>
> Power of storm be yours,
> Power of moon be yours,
> Power of sun.
>
> Power of sea be yours,
> Power of land be yours,
> Power of heaven.
>
> Goodness of sea be yours,
> Goodness of earth be yours,
> Goodness of heaven.
>
> Each day be joyous to you,
> No day be grievous to you,
> Honour and compassion.
>
> Love of each face be yours,
> Death on pillow be yours,
> The Saviour with you.[4]

A young woman on Islay explained how the new school system could belittle the traditional Gaelic culture. When she came as a schoolgirl to the island she was delighted to hear her sister schoolgirls' endless flow of Gaelic songs and stories, but if the schoolmaster caught any of them singing in the Gaelic on their way home from school he would call them back and cane them "till the blood trickled from our fingers, although we were big girls, with the dawn of womanhood upon us; the thought of that scene thrills me with indignation."[5]

From the prayers and poems and stories collected by Carmichael in the *Carmina Gadelica,* I have tried to build up a picture of how these women interwove their Christianity with their everyday activities, with the passing of the seasons, and with the phases of life from birth to dying. Many of them seem to have had a continuing awareness of the intermingling of holy and ordinary, which they celebrated in a language that is always direct and personal. They speak to heaven and heaven speaks back to them in a wonderfully down-to-earth way, whether they are weaving the cloth for the household, blessing a child departing for the mainland, making poultices for bruised or bleeding knees, or baking the bread.

At first sight their lives may seem remote and distant from our modern concerns, when most of us live in towns or cities or in a countryside where the sense of community is fading fast. But they have much to teach us about our relationships with other people and with the natural world. They can show us how to do ordinary things in a spirit of celebration that comes from a sense of being connected with the flow of humanity, the life energies. They can remind us of the sense of place and community that we are in danger of losing when we increasingly live privatized lives without reaching out to other people (especially other people who are not like us). For in traditional communities based on place people learned to tolerate or even appreciate neighbours of different ages, skills and temperaments, and they looked after them in times of need.

There seems to be in these lives a hospitality to human and divine which warns of the dangers of building our own cosy burrows and cutting ourselves off from the human warmth of dialogue and relationship because we are afraid of the risks of hurt and pain that may come of human relationships. There is, too, a strong focus on keeping the house as the centre of everybody's lives, a place of warmth and comfort and support in good and bad times. The household in the Gaelic culture was the centre of the world, the place of work and entertainment, where birthing and loving and learning and nurturing went on, as well as quarrelling and suffering and dying. Even heaven was seen as a kind of ultimate household up above, with the angels and saints (depending whether you were Protestant or Catholic) behaving like kindly and amiable friends and neighbours.

The woman of the house would not have been able to say, as now some women apologetically say, "I'm only a housewife," for she was at the heart of living and of the community, and the distinctions between private and public were not as sharply defined as they are in our society, where too often public work is valued at the expense of the work done at home of passing on values to children, and giving them models of human warmth and mutual help. It is no answer to urge that women should give up working outside the home, as the majority of women now do because they need the money and a sense of contact with the world beyond the domestic. Nor is it an answer to undervalue the domestic, as some schools of feminism do, believing that women's self-fulfilment depends on engagement with the public world. What is needed is a way of seeing the public and private as one world, where women and men have distinctive contributions to make to both spheres. This means revaluing the household so that women and men both make time to share the everyday ordinary occasions (mealtimes, outings, bathing the children, looking after the sick and the elderly). It means extending private mothering and nurturing to the public world of organizations and government, so that there is greater use of the qualities that women consider more important than men, but find difficult to express in many male-oriented public activities. This kind of public mothering would involve some of the old community behaviour which is characteristic of the Gaelic culture — taking account of the personal impact of public activities, putting abstractions in their grass roots context, aiming for a convivial dialogue rather than fluent dogma and aggressive confrontation.

Conviviality has a special significance in this Gaelic folk Christianity, which conventional religion often loses. These women address their prayers to the family of heaven on friendly and mutual terms: "Bless You to me my eye, and may my eye bless all it sees." God the Father may be King and Lord, but he is more like the clan chief or a local prince of the Celtic world than an awe-inspiring monarch of an oppressive nation state. A vital expression of this conviviality is the celebration of daily routines as simple as getting up and lighting the fire, or sacramentally breaking a harvest or Christmas cake and sharing it among the household. But it extends beyond the immediate household to include neighbours and strangers too, though the latter might be viewed with suspicion till their business was known. A widely used Celtic rune of hospitality goes like this:

> We saw a stranger yesterday,
> We put food in the eating place,
> Drink in the drinking place,
> Music in the listening place,
> And with the sacred name of the Triune God
> We were blessed, and our house,
> Our cattle and our dear ones.
> As the lark says in her song:
> Often, often, often goes the Christ
> In the stranger's guise.

That rune displays the Gaelic gift of retelling the Bible stories in their own words and relocating them in their own place. Bethlehem is still Bethlehem, but the setting is transformed to bear a detailed resemblance to the Western Isles, and the serving-woman at the inn is now the much-loved St Brigid, who makes up for the poor hospitality offered to Mary and Joseph by giving them her own bannocks, and later being Mary's midwife at the birth of Jesus. The Christian message is born anew in their own time and place, to answer to their own condition.

Personal expression lies at the heart of Gaelic spirituality. The people take direct responsibility for their spiritual lives, and every day of the year they give voice to their hopes and fears, their sufferings and their celebrations. Maybe this was in part the result of being left to their own spiritual resources for long periods when ministers and priests did not visit the remoter island communities because of the travelling difficulties. But this very remoteness also meant that their Christianity retained elements of the old druidical paganism that preceded it. The women's baptism of new born babies which persisted alongside church baptism shows signs of its pagan heritage. It includes a safeguarding from the fays, and refers to the three waves or the nine wavelets, reiterating the magic triad of the Celts which predated the Christian Trinity. Whatever the reasons for such creative deviations from standard Christian liturgies and sacraments, they show us the possibilities of shaping a lay spirituality, of creating moving ceremonies for our rites of passage, using our own words and our own energies to celebrate everyday occasions.

Pagan formulae are embedded, too, in some of the healing prayers and runes that accompany Gaelic herbal remedies. Belief in good and bad magic continued to exist alongside Christian beliefs in the healing God. There was a strong sense that the whole person needed healing and not just the part that showed symptoms of disease. This resonates with more progressive modern views, especially those of alternative medicine, which emphasise the connections between physical symptoms and the sufferer's state of mind and heart and life style. A North Uist woman healer said that "She knew immediately on beginning her prayer whether the illness was due to natural causes or to the evil eye. In the former event she prescribed herbal remedies; in the latter she countered it through prayer."[6] In some cases it seems that miraculous results were obtained by folk healers, but the question of magic and miracles has always been a difficult one for Christianity. According to some interpretations of the New Testament, Matthew and Luke modified or omitted stories about Jesus' miracle-working, because they did not want him to appear as a pagan wonder-worker or shaman. The trouble with miracles is that they can be evidence of cheap magic-working powers, or of genuine divine healing, and who is to set themselves up as judge of such matters?

The early Celtic saints like Brigid and Columba seem to have had no inhibitions about miracle-working, if we believe their medieval chroniclers. The *Carmina Gadelica* confirms the Gaelic faith in saintly miracles, and in the ability of the Celtic saints to transcend the boundaries of time and space in order to converse with and assist the ordinary people of the Highlands and Islands. It is clear that in the early days of Celtic Christianity the saints had to outdruid the druids as wonder-working healers and conjurors of the elements, the winds and the waves in particular, as befits a seabound and lochan-dotted land. Otherwise conversions would have been few among the ordinary people. The early reputations for miracle working continued through the centuries little tarnished, for the shepherd of Coigeach, Roderick MacLeod, told Carmichael with great conviction that "Columba had power to heal humans and cattle and horses and goats. There was no healer in Scotland nor in Ireland nor in any part of the world who could excel his hand ... He walked in the way of God and of Christ every step that he took, each place he was in."[7]

That story leads to a vital aspect of this culture that may have something important to say to our own restless and sceptical era. A sense of continuity between present and past, a sense of having roots in one's own place which are part of one's self-identity, are pervasive in the *Carmina Gadelica*. The search for substitutes for the communities we have lost goes on unabated today in urban areas and in the countryside, too, where agribusiness wastes and heritage parks continue to render redundant rural dwellers who might retain an inkling of the meaning of community. These Gaelic songs remind us of the basic human need for community, but it is no good fleeing to the Outer Hebrides or its equivalent in nostalgic evasion of the modern world. There is, in any case, a Ministry of Defence rocket range in Benbecula, whose radar aerials reach higher to heaven than the huge modern sculpture of the Mary Mother lower down the hillside. The English-speaking personnel dilute the remnants of the Gaelic-speaking community, but the rocket range provides jobs for the locals and helps to stem the flow of emigration.

For the majority of people who do not grow up with a sense of community based on place, it is necessary to work at community with whatever tools we can resourcefully discover. Our spirituality has to find expression in our communities of work, of social commitment, of family and friends, of neighbours and leisure activities. If we seek to heal the splits between male and female, private and public, personal and political, human and natural creation, we need to go on a kind of Celtic vision quest for full humanity. We may well discover the meaning of community along the way, if we can manage "to grow in sensitivity to self, to other people, to the non-human creation and to God or Big Consciousness," as Ursula King describes the process.

The fruits of Gaelic spirituality can help us on our vision quest, if we look beneath the surface differences between their way of life and our own, and concentrate on their rootedness in ordinary everyday life, their capacity for seeing the connectedness of everything rather than the separateness, their hospitality to other people and to the household of heaven. As Carmichael noted in his introduction to the *Carmina Gadelica,* these Gaels were "sympathetic and synthetic [i.e. synthesizing], unable to see and careless to know where the secular began and the religious ended."[8] Their prayers and blessings are "the product of far-away thinking, come down on the long stream of time. Who the thinkers and whence the stream, who can tell? Some of the hymns may have been composed within the cloistered cells of Derry and Iona, and some of the incantations among the cromlechs of Stonehenge and the standing stones of Callarnis."

1. Woman of the house

The house was the true focus of everyday life for man, woman, children and livestock in the old Gaelic way of life, for there was no separation of work from the rest of life, nor separation of the individual from community. The crofting township was a scattering of croft houses each in its own smallholding, a piece of land big enough to keep the household in potatoes, carrots and kail, with space for a hen run. Crofting was communal, so each crofter had rights to keep a cow or two on township grazings, to run sheep on the hill pasture, and to cut peats in early summer from the moorland.

The women spun and dyed the wool from the sheep, and wove and sewed to make the family clothes and provide the house with blankets. They made butter and cheese, hatched out chickens, and in some remote places went on grinding their own grain between quern stones for the baking flour. Home remedies were concocted from the herbs that grew in the locality, and administered with a mixture of Christian blessing and pagan rune to make doubly sure of effective healing. The children learned by listening and helping the grown-ups in the daily work, in some cases having charge of their own chickens or their own lambs, and competing with the other children to have the best looked-after farm animals in their township.

Celebrating everyday tasks

Everyday ordinary activities were often accompanied by their own special prayers and blessings, for there was no clear distinction made in this organic way of life between sacred and secular, spiritual and practical. The people themselves shaped the oral tradition of work songs and handed them down from one generation to another, not as a dead heritage but as a

continuing celebration of the daily and seasonal cycles of work.
They had ceremonies for every phase of the life cycle, too, from
birth to death, and these were often carried out by lay people,
for priests were few and far between in the remote communities
of the Western Isles. This meant that Christian rites of passage
were overlaid on ancient pagan invocations, as in the baptism by
the "knee-woman" or midwife which safeguarded the new-born
from the fays until the formal church baptism could take place.

The centrality of the household carried over into the Gaelic
way of seeing the Christian faith. Heaven was the household on
high, peopled by friendly saints and angels, who could be
addressed personally in daily conversation, and asked for help
in the everyday tasks and crises of life. God was King of the
Elements, of sun and moon and stars, of fire and water and
earth and air, all of which had their practical uses in running
the earthly household. Every member of the house had their own
guardian angel to watch over them in sleep and to bear them up
to their home in heaven when they died. Stories from the
Scriptures were retold in the context of their own familiar
everyday lives in the crofting townships. So when Christ was
pursued by his enemies he was concealed by a crofter beneath
a heap of grain to save him, and the God who divided the Red
Sea to make a safe pathway for the children of Israel is the
same God who is invoked to bring the men safely home from the
fishing when the Atlantic waters of the Minch turn stormy and
dangerous. The story of the five loaves and the two fishes that
Jesus made into a miraculous feast becomes a down-to-earth
grace before meals that reminds of the need for everyday
sharing of scarce food:

> May the blessing of the five loaves and the two fishes
> which our God shared out among the five thousand be
> ours. May the King who did the sharing bless our own
> sharing out and our sharing with each other.

The woman of the house was not, like some modern housewives,
disparaged as someone on the fringes of real life and real work,
cut off from the things that matter in the larger world. She
found self-expression not only in the traditional roles that

Christianity has assigned to women, as wives and mothers and angels at the hearth, but as a significant worker in the community economy. She was literally the maker of the daily bread, the spinner and weaver of the household clothes. She carried the peats home from the moorland in a wicker creel strapped to her back, often carrying her baby as well on the long miles between peat cuttings and croft.

The striking aspect of her unending activity is that she could find meaning and purpose in everything she did, thanks to the interweaving of pagan and Christian traditions which sustained her every day from her getting up to her lying down. There is a sense of belonging to the community by contributing to its sustenance, and by sharing experiences with neighbour women, as she goes about her ordinary tasks. Nor was it all sweetness and light, for life in the Western Isles was always hard-won and fraught with shortages and sickness and exile of self or children from the beloved place of belonging. These contingencies were endured with a practical resilience and had their own special prayers and blessings — for children leaving home or for sickness in the household, of people or livestock.

Always the household fire stood as a symbol of continuing life and renewed energy, and it was the first task of the woman of the house on getting up to bring the fire back to life and to meditate literally on hearth and home.

Blessing the household fire

The household fire was more than a practical convenience for cooking the food and drying out clothes and keeping the family warm. It was a reminder of the flame of life, of the need to rekindle basic energies every day of our lives, to keep in touch with our inner life force and avoid apathy and coldness in ourselves or towards others. So the fire was never allowed to go out, except on the May Day festival of Beltane, when all the fires were extinguished and rekindled from the community fire lit on the top of a hillock in each township as an annual ritual of purification and renewal in community.

They had many songs for blessing the home fire, but the

following three show particularly well how close and personal was the spiritual to the daily round of housework that had to be repeated day after day, but could nevertheless be given meaning far beyond drudgery.

Blessing of the kindling

I will kindle my fire this morning
In presence of the holy angels of heaven,
In presence of Ariel of the loveliest form,
In presence of Uriel of the myriad charms,
Without malice, without jealousy, without envy,
Without fear, without terror of anyone under the sun,
But with the Holy Son of God to encircle me.
Without malice, without jealousy, without envy,
Without fear, without terror of anyone under the sun,
But with the Holy Son of God to encircle me.

God, kindle you in my heart within me
A flame of love to my neighbour,
To my foe, to my friend, to my kindred all,
To the brave, to the bad, to the coward,
O Son of the loveliest Mary,
From the lowliest thing that lives
To the name that is highest of all.
    O Son of the loveliest Mary,
    From the lowliest thing that lives
    To the name that is highest of all.[1]

Last thing at night the woman of the house banked down the fire, smothering or "smooring" the embers with just enough ashes to keep the fire smouldering overnight, but not enough to put it out, for that would bring ill fortune. In many of the old black houses the embers were raked into a circle divided into three sections by bits of peat to represent the protection of the Trinity, before they were covered with peat ash.

Blessing the night fire (1)

I will build the hearth
As Mary would build it.
The encompassing of Bride and of Mary
Be safeguarding the hearth, safeguarding the floor,
Safeguarding the household all.

Who are they on the grass outside?
Michael the sun-radiant of my trust.
Who are they on the middle of the floor?
John and Peter and Paul.
Who are they by the end of my bed?
Sun-bright Mary and her son.

The mouth of God promised,
The angel of God proclaimed
An angel white in charge of the hearth
Till white day shall come to the embers,
    An angel white in charge of the hearth
    Till white day shall come to the embers.[2]

Blessing the night fire (2)

I smother the fire this night in three
Like the son of Mary would, before sleep.
God be encircling the peats and the fire to be,
God be encircling the company entire.

God be encircling us and holding us,
God be encircling us all in our sleep.
God be encircling the flocks of the fold,
God be encircling the hearth to keep it.

Who is keeping night watch now for me and mine?
Who but Christ of the poor is here,
And bright white Bride of the cattle,
And bright white Mary of the curly hair.

Safe be the house and safe be the stock,
Safe be the son and safe be the daughter,
Safe be the woman of the house and her man,
Safe be the household all that is here.[3]

Ending the day

The final prayer of the day before going to sleep was to ask the Being of Life not to withold His sustaining light, even though the plain daylight had gone. The protection of the Trinity and the saints through the hours of darkness was invoked in a personal and mutual way. The heavenly household is present in the earthly house, like longed for and welcome guests who give their warmth and safeguarding, just as the people of the house offer their own simple hospitality to the heavenly ones. There is hospitality and warmth offered by both human and divine people, an obligation on both sides, even if the divine hospitality is never-failing and without stint, while human hospitality is well known to suffer its ups and downs and its partialities.

Lying-down blessing

I am lying down tonight
With bright Mary and her Son,
With pure-white Michael,
And with Bride, beneath her cloak.

I am lying down with God,
And God will lie down with me,
I will not be lying down with Satan,
Nor shall Satan lie down with me.

O God of the poor,
Help you me this night,
Do not leave me entirely
From your house of treasures ...[4]

In some of the lying-down blessings, ancient beliefs emerge about the soul leaving the body during sleep and flying with the hosts of the air, which might be angels of light or angels of darkness, depending on the kind of life led by the sleeper. The guardian angel of the better sort would sweep the sleeping soul up to the gates of heaven to have a foretaste of the delights awaiting them there, while the dark angel would descend with the worse sort of person to the gates of hell to warn them of the wailings and miseries awaiting the damned.

These beliefs in the hosts of the air link up with the widespread medieval imaginings about the Wild Hunt that spread across Europe between the ninth and fourteenth centuries. The Wild Hunt was a ghostly cavalcade that swept up the souls of the sleeping and carried them off to nocturnal revelries. It might be seen as a benign troup of women led by a shining being often identified with Diana the Roman goddess of the hunt, or it could be a devilish horde led by Herodias, the wicked woman of the New Testament. Those who believed literally in such goings on were condemned by the Church as deluded by demons, and accusations of witchcraft could be the result of careless imaginings about the hosts of the air, right up to the seventeenth century in Scotland, when the last witch burnings took place.

In a few of the lying-down prayers in the Western Isles there seem to be remnants of this earlier consciousness about the dangers of being snatched up during sleep and carried off for good or evil by ambiguous hosts of the air:

Guardian Angel

O guardian angel of my right hand,
Be you with me this night,
Save me in the battling floods,
Wrap me in your linen, for I am naked,
Safeguard me, for I am feeble and forlorn.

Steer you my coracle in the crooked eddies,
Guide you my step in gap and pit,
Guard me in the treacherous turnings,

> And rescue me from the harm of the wicked,
> Rescue me from the harm of the wicked.
>
> Drive off from me the taint of pollution,
> Encompass me till Doom from evil,
> O kindly angel of my right hand,
> Deliver you me from the wicked this night,
> Deliver you me this night.[5]

If the forces of evil were imagined as very real and menacing, they could be counteracted by the forces of good. So the dark hosts could be kept at bay by the white hosts, the guardian angels sent by God to be the friendly protectors of individual, household and community, as the need arose. In a Christmas carol one of the islanders imagines the white host offering friendship:

> I see the hills, I see the strand,
> I see the host upon the wing,
> I see angels on the clouds,
> Coming with speech and friendship to us.[6]

And in a night prayer, another visualizes the need for protection:

> God, give charge to your blessed angels,
> To keep guard around this house tonight,
> A band consecrated, hearty and brave,
> That will shield this soul-shrine from harm.[7]

But protection by the white hosts meant also positive guidance, as well as warding off evil, as in this prayer to a guardian angel:

> Be you a bright flame before me,
> Be you a guiding star above me,
> Be you a smooth path below me,
> And be a kindly shepherd behind me,
> Today, tonight, and for ever.[8]

Women's work

Dairying

Lowland farmers, it used to be said, were reluctant to buy island cows because they would not yield their milk without their favourite songs being crooned to them by the milker. It seems that young women who got work as milkmaids in the Western Isles had to have good voices and a sense of the joy of life, as well as the elements of milking skills. Carmichael paints a highly romantic picture of the scene at the pasture when the bigger herds were being milked at the grazings, rather than being brought in to the byres:

> ... three or four comely girls among a fold of sixty, eighty or a hundred picturesque highland cows on meadow or mountain slope. The moaning and heaving of the sea afar, the swish of the wave on the shore, the carolling of the lark in the sky, the unbroken song of the mavis on the rock, the broken melody of the merle in the brake, the lowing of the kine without, the response of the calves within the fold, the singing of the milkmaids in unison with the movement of their hands and of the soft sound of the snowy milk falling into the pail, the gilding of hill and dale, the glowing of the distant ocean beyond, as the sun sinks into the sea of golden glory ...[9]

In the usual way of things the ordinary household would have only one or two cows, and they would be taken out to pasture in the morning and brought back in again for the evening milking. But however few or many, the herd would be put under the daily safeguarding of St Brigid, for she was regarded as a kind of divine milkmaid among her many other attributes. She was the one to give them protection and to bless them with fertility, if her aid was summoned.

Herding blessing

I will place this herd before me,
As was ordained by the King of the World,
Brigid to keep them, to watch them, to tend them,
On ben, in glen, on plain;
Brigid to keep them, to watch them, to tend them,
On ben, in glen, on plain.

Arise, you Brigid, the gentle and fair,
Take you your lint, your comb and your hair,
Since you made to them the lovely charm
To keep them from straying, to save them from harm;
Since you made to them the lovely charm
To keep them from straying, to save them from harm.

From the rocks, from the drifts, from the streams,
From crooked passes, from destroying pits,
From the straight arrows of the slender banshee,
From the heart of envy, from the eye of evil;
From the straight arrows of the slender banshee,
From the heart of envy, from the eye of evil.

Mary Mother, tend you the offspring all,
Fair-handed Brigid, encompass my herd,
Kindly Columba, saint of many powers,
Nurture the cow mothers to bring me more beasts.
Kindly Columba, saint of many powers,
Nurture the cow mothers, to bring me more beasts.[10]

In pleas for protecting and safeguarding livestock, Brigid, Mary
and Columba are frequently addressed — Mary as all nurturing
mother, Brigid as Christ's foster mother and divine milkmaid,
and Columba because he was Christ's Druid and Christ was his
Druid. Till the nineteenth century Columba was remembered
with personal affection as if he had only recently gone, and not
thirteen hundred years before. The blurring of pagan and Christian elements in stories about Columba gave him a double healing edge, since stories were told of him bettering the pagan

druids at their own magic, while bringing new Christian spells
into use as well. In the following tale of Columba's healing of
livestock (told by a woman in Barra), there may be a hidden
moral on the need to replace pagan spells with Christian
blessings. A poor widow woman begged Columba to restore the
cow's milk yield, so that she could give milk to her hungry
children and to the calf:

> Colum Cille said to the poor little woman: "I have made
> cow spells and horse incantations in my day and in my
> generation. I had them in a skin book and I had the skin
> book in the window. The skin book was stolen from me,
> and I lost the charms for cows and the spells for horses
> — but I will make a rune for you, you poor dear woman,
> for you to sing to your heifer, and before you have fin-
> ished the rune the little heifer will have taken to her calf
> ..." And Columba sang the charm to the poor dear
> woman, with the tears streaming down his cheeks.[11]

And the cow was of course moved to give her milk again, for not
only had Columba miraculous healing powers, but he had too
that gift highly prized in oral cultures — the gift of eloquence.
He was "the best at speaking and the best at singing and the
best at melody that was born of woman."

In buttermaking as in herding, Mary, Brigid and Columba
were called upon for direct personal help, as if they were rather
special neighbours who had stepped out of the Scriptures and
were quite at home in the Western Isles:

Butter making

> Come, you Colum Cille kindly,
> Hasten the lustre on the cream;
> Look you at the neglected orphans,
> Waiting the blessing of the cow's milk-wave?
> (Send down the broken, and bring up the whole.)
>
> Come, you Brigid, helper calm,
> Hasten the butter on the cream;

Look you at yon impatient Peter
Waiting the buttered bannock, yellow and white?
(Send down the broken, and bring up the whole.)

Come, you Mary Mother mild,
Hasten the butter on the cream;
Look you at Paul and John and Jesus
Waiting the gracious butter there.
(Send down the broken, and bring up the whole.)[12]

In this as in other poems, the Bible characters belong to the Gaelic communities, so there is no problem making the messages of Christianity real and vivid to everyday lives. This is a striking and endearing way of making the lessons about compassion and helping neighbours take root in the community's own life style. In the Gaelic retelling of the Flight into Egypt, Mary is tired out from the journey and asks a woman who is on her way to milk the cows if she will hold the baby Jesus for a while and give Mary a chance to rest. The woman selfishly refuses and rushes off to get on with her milking. Then a second milkmaid comes by who is happy to stop and play with the baby Jesus and sing him songs while Mary rests. Although she is late milking the cows because she put her own convenience second to her sister-woman's needs, she finds that her cows are giving her twice as much milk as usual in half the time.

Calanas or wool-working

Calanas was the whole process from washing, combing and carding the raw wool, through spinning and dyeing, to weaving and finishing or waulking the final cloth. There was an element of competitive rivalry between neighbour women, and they sometimes met in each others' houses to hold spinning competitions among themselves. These were sociable occasions as well, and so was the communal effort of finishing the cloth, the waulking process, when a group of up to a dozen women would be seated around a trestle table working at a length of newly woven tweed, but usually turning the occasion into a singing match and a chance for a good gossip.

The *calanas* was a test of excellence for the woman of the house. The woman unskilled or clumsy and slow at the wool working was often the butt of community jibes. Her family would be catching their deaths from want of warm clothing, or, as they said in Uist: "Swift in winter is the man of the *corra-chrosdag* in crossing the *machair*."

During the winter months the women worked early and late at the wool, the mothers and grandmothers teaching their own skills to the daughters, from the time they were little girls. When this failed to happen, as a result of death or careless inattention to a girl's upbringing, the unfortunate girl would be in trouble, as the following story shows:

A young woman was in disgrace with her husband's mother and sisters because she was found to be no good at carding and spinning and weaving. She lay awake night after night beside her sleeping husband, worried sick about her shortcomings, till her mother came back to her in a dream and promised to teach her everything she needed to know if she could only stay awake every night and apply herself heart and soul to the learning. So she worked every single night beside her dream mother, only retiring to sleep with Mary's lark and rising again with the first crow of the old cock, so that not even her husband knew of her night's work through the long winter.

The dream mother saved the young woman's face with her in-laws, and at last she had the skills that everywoman was respected for in that community of time and place. Before she was a mother for the first time, the story ends, she had made tartans and plaids and blankets that they had never seen the like of before, and they accepted her for one of themselves.

The power of the *cuigeal,* the distaff, was held in awe, and to be worthy of wielding that power a woman had to develop her skills till she "could make a shirt of mountain down for her lover and a pair of stockings for herself." Then she was considered a fit woman of the house and given standing among the others in the sisterhood of the woolworking, and trusted to use her distaff power with care and discretion. The distaff was literally a rod with a three-pronged end that was, according to legend, "always in the hands of the women, in and out, at home or abroad," and moreover "represents the Holy Trinity." They said that a boy or a male beast should never be struck with the distaff, in case it deprived them of their potency.

In dyeing the wool the woman of the house used natural plant colours collected from moorland and seashore where she lived. The rock-growing crotal has minute blood-red flowers that provided a bright true red dye. The root of the white-flowering water-lily was boiled to give a lustrous blackness when mixed with alum, and this was in common use for jerseys and pullovers. Gathering the water-lilies from the numerous moorland lochans needed strength and resolution, for the gnarled roots were tough and difficult to cut, and non-swimmers could get close to drowning in the process. Still, there was also the possibility of romantic encounters, as a young man's lyric recalls:

> A day that I was crossing the cold mountains, I came
> upon a young woman. She was deep to her two hips
> pulling the water lilies.

The first step in weaving was to work the pattern, plain or tartan, in the different coloured threads on a small piece of wooden board. Then the web was warped, preferably on a Thursday, for that is St Columba's day and auspicious for starting an important enterprise like a new web of cloth. The woman of the house would sing the chant of the warping to bless the new work, and to protect the sett from evil eye and the bad-mouthing of ill-disposed persons. She prayed for herself and her work to be encircled by the safeguarding of the High King, of Mary and her shepherd Son, of Brigid the companion woman of all women.

The complicated colours and patterns of some of the tartans were memorized by putting them into song, as in this extract from a North Uist warping chant:

Thursday excelling
For warping and fulling,
Ten fifteens telling
For pulling.

Brightest blue thread-strand,
Two white surrounding,
And scarlet a fiery band
For bounding.

Warp even setting,
God give me blessing,
All in my steading
Encompassing.[13]

While the cloth was on the loom it was protected from mischief
while lying idle over the sabbath. On Saturday night the woman
tied up her loom and sang a loom blessing over it:

Bless, my Chief of generous chiefs,
My loom and all things near to me,
Bless me in all I do,
Keep you me safe all my life.

From every brownie and banshee,
From every wicked wish and grief,
Be aiding me, Being of Aiding,
While I am here in the land of the living.

In Mary's name, her mild in deeds,
In Columba's name, the potent doer,
Keep holy the four posts of my loom
Till I start up again on Monday.

The pedals, the sleay and the shuttle,
The reeds, the warp and the cogs,
The cloth beam and the thread beam,
The thrum ends and the twined thread ply.

Each web of black and white and fair,
Of roan and dun and checked and red,
On every spot your blessing be,
On every shuttle under every thread,

So be my loom unharmed to last
Till Monday and I rising from rest,
Fair Mary will be giving me her love
And there'll be nothing that I cannot best.[14]

When the weaving was completed the waulking or finishing of
the length of cloth would follow. The women sat together round
a trestle and dragged and pulled and pounded the cloth to and
fro, from end to end and from side to side, to stretch it and beat
it into shape. They had a rich repertoire of waulking songs to
keep the otherwise dull work going on sociably and good-
humouredly. However repetitious the actual tasks, they were
made not just tolerable but turned into a special occasion by the
company and the talk, the laughing and singing. Songs changed
and were adapted to incorporate local scandal and gossip,
according to the ingenuity of the women around the table, but
there was care not to exceed the bounds, for fear of ill omens on
the web of cloth. So there was an element of ceremony to ensure
that the high-spirited spontaneity did not get out of hand.

There were three leading women to guide the waulking — the
woman of waulking to superintend the quality of the work, the
woman of the songs to keep watch over the quality of the singing, and the third to ensure that no bad omen was in danger of
coming on the cloth as a result of breaking taboos (singing the
same song twice, or one woman's voice drowning out her companions' voices by her loud screeching). As the web emerged
finally in good shape and with the nap rising, the three leading
women would take it in turns to bless the finished cloth. Each
would turn round in a circle while holding the web and would
say: "I give a turn, sunwise, in the name of the Father/the
Son/the Holy Spirit." Sometimes the web was passed round the
table sunwise, and each woman there would give it her own
well-wishing turn and bless it for whoever would be its user,
saying:

> This is not second-hand cloth,
> This cloth is not begged,
> This is no belongings of cleric or priest ...
>
> It is cloth for my beloved child Catherine/
>   my companion beloved John.[15]

"Each member of the household for whom the cloth is intended is solemnly mentioned by name in the consecration," Alexander Carmichael observed. During his travels in the Western Isles collecting the Gaelic lore, he was present on many an occasion at the waulking, and was much moved by the liveliness and wit of the women's singing. The young ones would sometimes engage in singing exchanges about the merits and demerits of each other's lovers, which were much appreciated by the whole group in a community where everyone knew personally who was being praised or satirized.

When it came to the consecration of the cloth however the mood changed and all became serious, as one of the three leading women, the "celebrant," led the rest in chanting in unison a blessing that was both a blessing on the cloth and on those who would wear the cloth.

> May the man of this clothing never be wounded,
> May torn he never be;
> The time he goes into fight or affray,
> May the sanctuary shield of the Lord be his.
>
> The time he goes into fight or affray,
> May the sanctuary shield of the Lord be his.[16]

Quern songs

Hand-grinding meal between quern stones continued to be done into the latter half of the nineteenth century in remoter parts of the Western Isles, and the round quern stones the women used can often still be seen around the older croft houses, built into paths or gate posts, or used as garden ornaments. But even in Carmichael's time this slow and laborious job was giving way to the modern method of taking the grain to a mill for grinding. While it continued, however, women made the best of it by turning it into a sociable occasion between women and singing their songs to while away the monotony. Carmichael gives a vivid description of hand-grinding in a croft house in Barra, which he visited in January 1865:

Two women sat opposite each other on the floor with the quern between them. The right leg of each was stretched out, while the knee of the other leg formed a sharp angle, with the foot resting against the knee joint of the straight leg. A fan containing bere lay beside the women and from this one of them fed the quern, while the other relieved it of the constantly accumulating meal. Each woman held the handle with which they turned the quern, and as they turned they sang the quern blessing to a very pretty air. Then they sang an impromptu song for the stranger who was hungry and cold, and who was far from home and from the mother who loved him.

On Ash Eve

We shall have meat.
Yes we should have,
Yes we should have.

The cheek of hen,
Two bits of barley,
That would do us,
That would do us.

We shall have mead,
We shall have beer,
We shall have wine,
We shall have a feast.
We shall have sweetness and milk treats,
Honey and milk,
Wholesome brose,

Plenty of that,
Plenty of that.

We shall have hand harp,
We shall have pedal harp,
We shall have lute,
We shall have horn.
We shall have sweet psaltery
Of the melody strings,
And the queenly lyre
Of the songs we shall have,
Of the songs we shall have.

Calm fair Brigid will be with us,
Gentle Mary Mother will be with us.
Michael the Chief,
Of the glancing swords,
And the King of Kings
And Jesus Christ,
And the Spirit of peace
And of grace will be with us,
Of grace will be with us.[17]

Doing the baking

Gaelic women had ways of baking bread and cakes that show
how the most humdrum daily activity can be turned into a
celebration, given a bit of ceremony and a sense of special
occasions in the family or in the seasonal calendar, or both. The
woman of the house did a special baking for the Feast of St
Michael at the end of September, for example.[18] She mixed the
struan or Michael's cake from all the cereals grown on the farm,
moistened it with ewe's milk and covered it with layers of a
batter made of butter and eggs and cream while it was cooking
on the bakestone in front of the fire. It was the privilege of the
eldest daughter to take over the *struan* baking from her mother,
as soon as she was old enough to do it properly. The younger
children were made special little cakes of their own from a bit
of the mixture, to which honey, or caraway seed or blackberries

would be added, according to their favourite treats. Each child's miniature cake was blessed in the mixing, using the name of the child and saying: "Children and good fortune be to Catherine/ John ... and the mystery of Michael, and the safeguarding of the Lord." Each little cake would be cut out in a different shape which had a symbolic meaning. There was a three-cornered cake that stood for the Trinity, the five-sided for the Trinity and Mary and Joseph, the seven-sided for the seven mysteries, and the nine-sided for the nine archangels. A round cake was a symbol of eternity. Great care was taken during the making of the little cakes not to break the shape for that would bring ill luck and bad fortune on the baker and her family. If a cake was broken it could not be eaten, but had to be thrown out, in the hope that it could be forgotten, along with the ill omen that went with it.

There were mindful ways of treating leftover food including scraps from the baking board. At the St Michael's feast-day baking, the loose flour from the board was put in a footless stocking and sprinkled over the livestock the next day (St Michael's Feast proper) "to ward off from them the evil eye, mischance and the murrain." The livestock were part of the household too, and in need of similar blessings of fertility and thriving as the people. On ordinary days the treatment of leftover food was seen as significant too, and there were important customs to be observed. You gave away what was worth giving to those in the community whose resources were more meagre than your own, or who needed tiding over a bad patch caused by sickness or death in the family, or misfortune of cattle or crops.

What was left over from such almsgiving was the due of the Otherworld, the fairies, for "we must remember the smallest of God's creatures if we are to thrive in this world below and to live in the world beyond." So the scraps of dough that fell from the baking board and the crumbs that fell from the family table at mealtimes were the fairies' bits. It is not always clear whether such offerings were prompted by extended charity, or by fear of the fairies' spite if they were not propitiated. Fear of supernatural forces beyond one's control was not always eased by Christian beliefs since to ordinary people an all-powerful Father God in control of the universe does not square with the strokes of ill luck and bad fortune that can strike down a person or a household, whatever they do or do not do to deserve it. So the treatment of leftover food is an interesting blend of Christian charity and superstitious warding off of bad luck. They made sure to keep the people of the knoll sweet, as well as giving, those who could afford to, "a peck of meal, a quarter of *struan,* a quarter of lamb, a quarter of cheese and a platter of butter to the despised and rejected, to the almsworthy and to the orphans without pith, without power, formed in the image of the Father everlasting." Paying protection money to the pagan Otherworld was seen as a sensible precaution even in a Christian community, just in case ...

Looking after the hens

The woman of the house fed the hens, collected the eggs (or sent a careful child to do it for her) and set eggs for hatching. All these everyday jobs were done in a mindful way to avoid mishap and bring blessing on these creatures of the household and their produce. Thursday was often chosen for setting eggs to hatch, as it was Columba's day and he was regarded as a protector of the animal world. Friday was the worst day to do it, since that was the day of the Crucifixion. The choice of hens too was ruled by custom and belief. Speckled hens were thought superior to a single-coloured hen — less likely to leave their eggs, hardier than white hens and with more natural heart towards their chicks than black hens. Perhaps there was a connection with the old Celtic pagan idea that magic works best on the margins of two elements, where opposites meet and mingle.

The woman sang a hatching blessing as she went about setting the eggs under the speckled hen. It was both a prayer for protection and an oral culture's normal way of remembering the right way of carrying out a task. Putting instructions into verse and singing them is good mnemonics, and not as fossilizing as might first appear, for people in an oral culture are adept at impromptu responses and witty adaptations of songs handed down to them. Here is one of the hatching blessings which the women sang as they set the eggs.

Hatching blessing

I will rise early on Monday morning,
I will sing my rune and rhyme,
I will go sunwise with my cog
To the nest of my hen with purpose sure.

I will put my right hand on my breast,
My right hand to my heart,
I will ask for the kind wisdom of Him
Overflowing in offspring, broods and beasts.

I will close both my seeing eyes,
Like in blindman's buff moving slow;
I will stretch my left hand over there
To the nest of my hen on yonder side.

The first egg that I bring towards me
I will put widdershins round my head,
With my right hand into the cog set by,
And there in the cog shall be one.

I will lift up my left hand again
I will stretch out without a pause,
I will bring the two eggs down here,
And there'll be three in the cog.

My right hand I'll stretch out again,
I'll lift with it three at a time,
I'll ask the guiding hand of the King,
And there'll be six in the clutch.

My left hand I'll reach out again,
I will bring four eggs down,
In the name of Christ, Chief of Power,
And there'll be ten in the cog.

The right hand has the stronger claim,
I'll lift two more with its fingers,

So to set my brood complete,
Under the breast of the big speckled hen.

I will mark their two ends with soot,
And I dumb as dumb the while,
In name of Creator of sea and hill,
In name of saints and apostles all.

In name of the Trinity, Holy Three,
In name of kindly Columba,
I will set the eggs on Thursday,
For a happy brood coming on a Friday.[19]

Working in the fields

Although men and women had their separate tasks on the croft,
there were times of the year when the whole family joined
together — to harvest the crops, and to get the peats in. Then
men, women and children would work through the long summer
days to beat the weather which was always capricious on those
Atlantic islands. Even so they found time for blessings and
thanksgiving ceremonies on their work.

At the beginning of harvesting the whole household dressed
in their best and went out into the field to thank the God of the
Harvest. The head of the house faced into the sun and cut the
first sickle of corn. Then he or she passed it three times sunwise
round their head, while starting up the reaping blessing, in
which everybody joined:

God, bless You Yourself my reaping,
Each ridge and plain and field,
Each sickle curved, crescent, honed,
Each ear and fistful in the sheaf;
Each sickle curved, crescent, honed,
Each ear and fistful in the sheaf.

Bless You each girl and lad,
Each woman and tender youngster,
Safeguard them under your shield of strength

And keep them in the house of the saints.
Safeguard them under your shield of strength
And keep them in the house of the saints.

Encompass You each goat and sheep,
Each cow and horse and store,
Encircle You the flocks and herds
And tend them to a kindly fold.
Encircle You the flocks and herds
And tend them to a kindly fold.

For the sake of Michael head of hosts,
Of Mary fair, branch of grace,
Of bright-white Brigid with the ringlets in her hair,
Of Columba of Iona's graves and tombs.
Of bright-white Brigid with the ringlets in her hair,
Of Columba of Iona's graves and tombs.[20]

Outdoor work and indoor work combined at certain seasons for the woman of the house in a seamless cycle of harvesting and consuming. Mary's feast day was celebrated on the fifteenth of August, and the woman of the house baked a special bannock that day from corn gathered in the field at dawn, dried in the sun on a rock, ground in a stone quern, kneaded in a sheepskin and baked on a fire of rowan or other sacred wood specially gathered by the family. She would break the bread and share it out among all present, while they sang the Praise of Mary, walking in procession round the central fire. Then they would go out of the house and walk sunwise round the steadings and the folds where the animals had been gathered in for the Mary blessing, everyone singing:

On the feast day of Mary the fragrant,
Mother of the Shepherd of the flocks,
I cut me a handful of the new corn,
I dried it gently in the sun,
I rubbed it sharply from the husk
With my own palms.

I ground it in a quern on Friday,
I baked it in a fan of sheepskin,
I toasted it by a fire of rowan,
And I shared it out round my people.

I went sunwise around my dwelling
In name of the Mary Mother
Who promised to keep me,
Who has kept me,
Who will keep me
In peace, in flocks,
In rightness of heart,
In labour, in affection,
In wisdom, in compassion,
For the sake of your Passion,
You Christ of Grace.
Who till the day of my death
Will never leave me,
    O till the day of my death
    Will never leave me.[21]

The first sheaf of the harvest was considered to be blest, and the last sheaf to be cursed, under the name of *A' chailleach* or the Hag. In many places there was great competition not to be the last person in the township to finish the harvest, for that meant supporting the invisible Hag all through the winter months of shortage. "Cattle-loss, death-loss and mischance" would be the lot of the last to finish. In some parts a man with all done would ride past his neighbour's uncompleted harvest field and fling the last sheaf into it. The insult of being given the Hag was not taken lightly, and if the bringer of the Hag was caught he would be stripped and clipped, "given the fool's tonsure," as the saying went, and sent back home naked.

This curse of the Hag in the form of the last sheaf contradicts the probably older veneration of the last sheaf as the symbol of the harvest safely gathered in. At country craft fairs today you can still find corn dollies celebrating the gathering of the harvest safely in, and offered with promises of fruitfulness and protective powers. The final sheaf is an ambiguous symbol, I suppose,

for ripeness and maturity are not far from decay and dying, so
the last sheaf can stand for fulfilment of promise and at the
same time the withering of fulfilment. But symbolic meanings
in close-knit communities are usually linked anyway with a
canny assessment of neighbours' well-doing or ill-doing ways, so
the thinking might be that the family tardiest at the harvesting
is the family that is generally ne'er-do-well and will not prosper.
There is no chance of hiding weaknesses in a country community, and the indigenous inhabitants rarely romanticize present
lives, however much they may be tempted to romanticize the
past.

Summer on the shieling

When Carmichael was collecting the lore of the Western Isles,
Lewis was the only place where the people still moved to the
shielings or mountain moorland pastures with their flocks
during the summer months, and he describes vividly the scene
in his idyll of the shieling:

> The shieling time is the most delightful time of the rural
> year, the time of the healthy heather bed and the healthy
> outdoor life, of the moorland breeze and the warm sun, of
> the curds and the cream of the heather milk. The young
> men come out from the townland in twos and threes and
> half-dozens to spend the night among the maidens of the
> shieling; some of them play the pipes or other instru-
> ment, and the song and the dance and the merriment
> begin and are continued all night long under the moon on
> the green grass before the shieling door.[22]

The summer life up at the shieling was a time when women,
children and animals were together while the men stayed below
in the townships repairing or rebuilding the house or steadings,
and going on with their fishing. The cattle and sheep grew fat
on the sweet mountain grasses, and the women made great
reserves of butter and cheeses. As usual they had their work
songs to sing — a blend of describing the task as if to hurry it
on, and of bringing down on the work the blessings of benign
beings, as in this butter-making charm:

The charm made of Columba
To the maiden of the glen,
Her butter to increase,
Her milk to make excelling.

Come, fat butter lumps, come!
Come, fat butter lumps, come!
Come, fat butter lumps, heaps of richness,
Come, fat butter lumps, come!

You who set shine in moon and sun,
You who set succour in seed and herd,
You who set fish in stream and seas,
Send up the butter soon!

Come, fat butter lumps, come!
Come, fat butter lumps, come!
Come, fat butter lumps, heaps of richness,
Come, fat butter lumps, come![23]

Becoming a woman of the house

When a girl grew up and was admitted to the company of
women, the occasion was celebrated as a significant rite of
passage, and she exchanged the young girl's hairband for the
white snood or kertch of the mature woman. Normally this was
the morning after her wedding, when the new woman of the
house would be reminded in song of the things she should aim
for in her new life, in order to win the respect of her community.
It was a time for celebration too, and a way for the new woman
of the house to be given the blessings of the others on her new
way of life, that she might enjoy good fortune in it and have
support and warmth to get started.

A thousand greetings to you, beneath your kertch,
Throughout your life course may you be whole.

Strength and days be yours in peace,
And bliss as well as means increase.

In starting your course of sharing, and you young,
In starting your race, seek you the God of life,
Fear not but He will rightly guide
Your every secret need and prayer.

Your wedding crown you now are wearing
Has often brought a grace to woman;
Good be in you, and grace with it,
And whiteness of word and deed.

Be you hospitable, yet be wise,
Be you courageous, but be calm,
Be you open and yet reserved,
Be you exact but generous.

Be not mean in your giving,
Do not flatter yet be not cold,
Speak not ill of neighbours, though ill they be,
If spoken of, show no resentment.

Be you careful of your name,
Be you dignified yet kind,
The hand of God be steering you,
In your willing, in your doing, in your thought.

When you bear a cross, be not a moaner,
When your cup is flowing, have a care!
Never to mischief give your hand —
Put on the kertch and welcome, woman of the house![24]

Naturally plenty of Gaelic women failed to live up to this
demanding set of ideals. In Ireland and Scotland to this day
such a one may be known as a "through other" woman, and in
the Gaelic she is called *riaslaisg,* "a woman who is always in
difficulties because of her untidy habits and unmethodical ways;
an unkempt, unwashed, slovenly woman." Another way of falling

short of the ideal was to be "she of the slippery gullet," the
relentless gossip who can keep no secret, and is always in and
out of her neighbours' houses, looking for more titbits of talk to
pass on, for she is addicted to tale-telling and loses nothing in
the telling so in the end she may become a truly malicious
mischief maker.

The worst woman of all was considered to be the inhospitable
woman of the house, for there was a belief that any stranger
who came up to your door was to be treated as if it were Christ
knocking. There was ordinary everyday compassion too for the
unfortunate who wandered the roads, often as a result of the
clearances, when they were too old or too ill to go on the emigrant ships to Canada. Even though the remaining crofters were
themselves impoverished, the tradition of hospitality lived on.
Many continued to share with those worse off than themselves,
and were critical of neighbours who shut their doors and turned
their back on the age-old sense of hospitality. This tradition was
not quite extinct in the early 1970s, for I remember one of the
last of the Highland tramps who was so well fed by the neighbour women that he was able to spend his dole money almost
entirely on whisky, and on updating the bicycle he used to
circulate from one hospitable homestead to another. He lived in
the interstices of two different cultures and enjoyed the benefits
of both.

The idea of hospitality in the Celtic lands seems to predate
the coming of Christianity with its ethos of compassion. The
pagan view was that those you shared food and drink with
were as members of your own household and could not be
harmed (though there were a number of notorious occasions
when the rule was broken, but they were considered so shocking that they reinforced the general precept). The presumption
was that travellers should be given food and shelter as if they
were part of the household, and not as any commercial trans-
action. While people shared food and drink they were expected
to be friends and to leave aside weapons and enmities, so the
hospitable meal was a way of reconciliation as well as a simply
convivial occasion for story telling and general enjoyment.
The pagan Celtic view of the Otherworld includes an amazing
amount of feasting and entertainment as a natural part of

the next life, with no guilt or sin attached, until the influence
of Christianity led to a more austere remodelling of the next
world.

Even after the coming of Christianity the early saints were
much given to performing miracles for the sake of conviviality
and hospitality, as if these were the spheres where they could
readily impress their new Gaelic converts. Many of St Brigid's
miracles fall into this category. She changed well-water into ale
for the sustenance of visiting clerics, and on another occasion
transformed a washing tub of dirty water into beer for bishops.
Her kitchen contained an ever renewable chunk of boiled bacon
which never diminished however many slices were cut off it for
the benefit of travelling strangers, the hungry poor and starving
hounds (for as usual the natural world is deserving of hospitality
as well as the human world).

The body of Brigid lore even includes what must be one of the
few known blessings on a kitchen. When her stepfather sent her
to the shieling to make butter, she gave it all away to the needy
and had to invoke the help of Jesus to fill up her kitchen again
when her stepfather demanded the produce:

> Oh, my Chief,
> Who can do all things,
> Bless, O God — a cry fair enough —
> My kitchen with your right hand.
>
> My kitchen,
> Be it the kitchen of the white God,
> A kitchen which my King has blessed,
> A kitchen full of butter![25]

Hospitality, however, was not extended foolishly to one and all,
without discrimination. "Be you hospitable, but be you wise,"
were the words used in blessing the new young woman of the
house. She had to learn to sift the needy from the greedy, to tell
the deserving from the spongers, and to know when enough was
enough. There was a certain degree of rationalization of prejud-
ice against certain groups, in particular the tinkers. It was a
tinker woman herself who told this story to Carmichael about

the tinkers' original sin that explained the bad treatment they got ever since the Crucifixion:

> After they had brought Christ to the cross, they found they had no nails to put into Him, nor any bellows to blow the fire to heat the iron to make nails. There is no knowing under the white sun what to say or what to do in the confusion that was there. But the tinker woman lifted her skirt and blew the fire, and the iron was heated, and the tinker man made the nails with which Christ was nailed to the tree of crucifixion. It was then that Jesus Christ the Son of the living and eternal God, up on the cross, said to the tinker woman down at the foot: "Thou and thy kind from generation to generation, from age to age, shall be walking the ways and travelling the wilderness, without rest of night, without peace of day, because of the work of thy hand and thine ill deed."[26]

The pervasive sense of hospitality which operated (with the exception of such examples of discrimination) in the Gaelic culture epitomizes the theme of this chapter — the centrality of home as secure haven, focus of warmth between people, and source of conviviality in good times as well as of comfort in bad times. The significance of the house was recognized in a house blessing which can be adapted for use today, on the occasion of moving house or renovating an old one:

> God bless the house
> From site to stay,
> From beam to wall,
> From butt to ben,
> From ridge to base,
> From balk to roof-tree,
> From founding to summit,
> Founding to summit.[27]

2. Woman of loving

Gaelic blessings for the people you loved were warmly given on all the everyday occasions where they might be needed, whether in times of celebration or of misery and sorrowing. They are striking because they start from the immediate situation of the person you are blessing, and visualize their experiences, and encircle those experiences with the protective blessing. Blessings are concrete rather than abstract, specific rather than generalized, personal and connecting rather than formal and distancing. They convey a sense of individual belonging to a chain of beings, where to receive a blessing is to have an obligation to do the same thing for someone else when the need arises.

Everyday affection

To sit down and eat a meal with the family or friends or a stranger (to whom hospitality was invariably offered) was a reminder of non-material as well as material need for food and drink and spiritual sustenance. The household of heaven was hovering in the background as a model for affectionate warmth and support, and however simple and plain the fare, it was a reminder of the harvest of the bountiful earth, as in this prayer of thanks for food:

> Give us, O God, of the morning meal,
> Good to the body, the frame of the soul.
> Give us, O God, of the seventh bread,
> Enough for our need at close of day.
>
> Give us, O God, of the honey-sweet foaming milk,
> The sap and sop of the fragrant farms,

And give us, O God, along with Your sleep,
Rest in the shade of Your Rock of the Covenant.

Give us this night of the meal that will last,
Give us this night of the drink without sorrow,
Give us this night, close to the heavens,
The chalice of mild Mary the kindly.

Be with us by day, be with us by night,
Be with us by light and by dark,
In our going to bed and our getting up,
In talk, in prayer, in walk.[1]

For family or friends setting out on a journey there were many
pilgrims' aiding songs to bless them in the hazards they might
go through, on land or on sea:

God be with you in every pass,
Jesus be with you on every hill,
Spirit be with you across each stream,
Headland and crest and grassy plain,

Each sea lane and land lane, each moor and meadow,
Each lying down, each getting up,
In the trough of the waves, on the ridge of the breakers,
Each step of the journey you are going.[2]

And for those undergoing a journey there were encompassing
blessings where the benighted traveller could get comfort by
following the same pattern of blessing learned at the affectionate
hearth of home:

God before me, God behind me,
God above me, God below me,
I on the path of God,
God on my track, too.

Who is there on the dry land?
Who is there on the bogland?

Who is there on the wave-strand?
Who is there by the door-jamb?
God and Lord.

Here I am — astray,
Here I am in strain,
Here I am in ruin,
Here I am in pain,
Here I am alone,
O God, encircle me.[3]

The basis for everyday affection in the old Gaelic culture was
taking things personally, seeing with the eyes of the heart as
well as with the eyes of the mind. This could lead to bitter
personal feuding and cursing in a close-knit community, but the
positive side was everyday attentiveness to individual need, a
practical desire to make people comfortable. By contrast our
dominant culture puts more value on distancing, on analysing
(taking apart rather than keeping together), and abstraction. A
good example of the Gaelic way of putting things personally and
bringing them down to everyday level is a prayer for peace
which puts the emphasis on individual relationships. It was
recited by Mary MacLeod of Gairloch:

Peace between neighbours,
Peace between kindred,
Peace between lovers,
In love of the King of Life.

Peace between person and person,
Peace between wife and husband,
Peace between woman and children,
The peace of Christ above all peace.

Bless, O Christ, my face,
Let my face bless everything;
Bless, O Christ, my eye,
Let my eye bless all it sees.[4]

Courting and loving

Love between the sexes in Gaelic life came under the influence of pagan and Christian views of women's role, and these were clearly in conflict. There are signs in the ceremonies for the Feast of Michael at the end of September that women had once taken more initiative in love-making than they were expected to do in a Christian society where the strictures of St Paul held sway, and female carnality was viewed with suspicion. On the Eve of St Michael young women went with their friends to dig up wild carrots to give to the men they fancied during the evening dancing. They would go into the dance house with their offerings, challenging the men with the traditional verses:

> Tis I myself am here with the carrots —
> Whoever he be that would get them from me;
>
> Tis I myself am here with the treasure —
> Whoever the hero could get them from me.[5]

The man would respond with traditional phrases like "Wifehood and fulfilment on my nut brown girl," or "Wifehood and the joy of dalliance and procreation on my girl." As the evening went on the girls replenished their supply of carrots from a secret store and returned to the dance with more offerings to their chosen men. The revelry continued into the following day when there would be horse racing and sunwise circuiting of the churchyard, with many a couple wandering off together to the sand dunes. The indications are that ancient pagan celebrations for the gathering in of the harvest continued on.

Other verses too suggest that women had at one time spoken openly and feelingly of their love longings, as the following two pieces show:

> Oh that I and my choice of partners were in yon glen up
> there, no witness beneath the white sun, save the bright
> star and the planets; no simple infant with no sense, no

gabbling one there nor lying one to spread about the story.[6]

> I would lie slenderly in the folds of your plaid,
> And at the end of the night come home again;
> I would put away my ribbons, folded,
> And I would fix the kerchief in proper mode.[7]

The latter refers to the custom of changing the maidenly hairband for the three-cornered kerchief of the mature woman, on betrothal or marriage. The woman of sexual maturity was called *brionnag*, bright or brilliant or glowing one, but this meaning was later used in a denigratory sense, to mean a flighty one, a giddy one, a light woman, as if female sexuality were something to be ashamed of and not something to celebrate.

The oldest love songs were often passed on from generation to generation of women around the trestle table while groups of women were waulking or finishing the webs of home-made tweed. Some of them are very sensuous in tone, probably retaining a pagan spirit, though the Song of Songs makes use of equally sensuous imagery in the Bible.

> O Apple tree, may God be with you,
> May the moon and the sun be with you,
> May the east and the west winds be with you,
> May everything that ever was be with you,
> May every bounty and desire be with you,
> May every passion and every divinity be with you,
> May great Somerled and his warrior band be with you,
> May everyone, and me myself, be with you.[8]

The reference to Somerled goes back to the Norse king who was Lord of the Isles in the eleventh century. In a version of the same poem from Islay a more austere Christian line replaces the open praise of bounty and desire: "May the Great Creator of the Elements be with you."

Some of the love songs conjure up the old Celtic hero tales where men must fight and women must weep at the slaughter and the loss of a lover. They depict a world where Finn MacCool

still strides the glens at the head of his warrior band, where the
ideal day for the hero is to stand with his mates in bloody
morning battle, and drink his fill in the evening, dallying with
fair women. The songs are put into the mouths of women, but
sometimes sound as if they were composed by men, since the
hero conventions are so dominant, as in this lament for a
missing lover:

Sleep has forsaken me

Sleep has forsaken me since Shrovetide,
Often I turn
In the hope of seeing your speeding ship
On blue-black ocean.

Surpassing swift your craft of grey timbers
From the slope of Lochlainn,
Every plank of her smooth as the swans' plumage
On the wavelets of a loch.

Out of Alba's three prime warriors one far faring,
This sorrows me sore,
Far afield without folk or dwelling
In the Isle of Man.

O King! If only the weight of your troubles
Were spread out over your land,
To every man his share, and on me
Full share of three.

Love of the lads are you on a morning early
In the front of the battle,
Love of the women in the laughter of evening
When harp is playing.

This I would ask, a blade in your right hand
In a narrow pass,
And you confronting the ones who hate you,
And blood blinding them.

There would come the carrion crow and raven
At the dawn's breaking,
Would drink their fill from the pools
Brimming, blood red.[9]

By contrast there are songs which seem to use women's own
feelings and interests, as in this St Kilda waulking song:

I would make the fine cloth for you,
Thread as stout as the rope of the thatch.

I would make the feathered slippers for you,
You loved and demanding of men.

I would give you the treasured anchor
And the gear in the house that my grandad had.

For my love is the hunter of the bird
The first to fly from foreign seas.

For my love is the master of the waves,
Great the joy will be in his face.[10]

And another tries to describe her longing in words natural to an
island woman:

It is not a lad I want,
But a fine man without stint,
A good hand to steer between the waves,
Be the wind north or south —
And a mighty favouring breeze
That would not hold us back.

Absent or missing lovers are a constant theme in these Gaelic
love songs. Even when there was no fighting going on between
the clans, and the memories of Norse invasions were fading from
the folk memory, men earned their living fishing notoriously
treacherous seas, or hunting gannets on the sheer cliffs for food
and oil, or ferrying cattle and sheep to island grazings across

swift tidal channels. At one time the women of St Kilda were left
with only one man among them, when the rest had gone sailing
to Boreray to bring back sheep, and were storm-stayed for
eighteen weeks. The women soon became dissatisfied with their
sole male companion Calum, and took to entertaining themselves at his expense. "They were making tunes and verses and
songs to him, one woman putting him down and another bringing him up, one woman dispraising him and another praising
him." It was a society where women developed strong bonds of
sisterly affection, and made their own entertainment, during the
frequent enforced absences of their men. But they kept their
men in their hearts all the same, composing many beautiful
songs of longing and lament, like this one, again from St Kilda:

> It was no crew of landsmen
> Crossed the ferry on Wednesday:
> Tis tidings of disaster if you're not alive.
>
> What has kept you so long from me
> In the high sea and the squalling wind catching you,
> So that you could not give her sail?
>
> 'Tis a journey with no winning
> That took the fine man away from me,
> To take our one son from me and from Donald.
>
> My son and three brothers are gone,
> And the only son of my mother's sister,
> And sorest tale told or to tell, my husband.
>
> It is this has set me to rake ashes,
> And to do a spell of digging —
> That the men are gone, and no word of their living.
>
> I am left without laughter or lightness,
> Sitting on the floor of the glen —
> My eyes are wet, many the tears on them.[11]

Rejection and jealousy

Alongside the romantic tone of love longings and love laments
there exists a quite different assortment of biting satirical
verses, covering the bitter disappointments of rejection by the
lover, or the hatred of a rival who has stolen the affections of the
beloved by usually unworthy means. These songs have a sharp
and witty bite which the romantic vein leaves untapped. They
relate to everyday feelings and a refusal to ignore the realities
of life, where a girl might be rejected not for herself but because
she had less material goods than her rival — but knowing that
is not much comfort when suffering the heart pangs of rejection.

These songs belong to an ancient Celtic tradition of satire,
where a person out of favour with the community might be
cursed by a poet — in certain cases cursed to death, such was
the power of the word in the Gaelic culture. Whatever the effect
of these gritty verses of insult on the recipient, they must have
had a therapeutic effect on the reciter at any rate. Satirical
abuse of this kind was often sung by the women around the
waulking table, and earlier pieces were adapted and wittily
transposed to bring in current gossip and the latest items.

Here is one example of letting off steam by a rejected young
woman:

> You girl there, may the sun turn against you!
> You have taken from me my autumn carrot,
> My Michaelmas carrot from my pillow,
> My lusty buck from among the goats.
>
> But if you have, it was not on your own,
> But with the black cunning of the dark women —
> You are the little she-goat that lifted the white linen,
> I am the little gentle cow that gave no milking.
>
> Stone in shoe be your bed to you,
> Dart in tooth be your sleep to you,
> Prickle in eye be your life to you,
> Uneasy watching by night and by day.

Be no little sleeper seen on your pillow,
Be no eyes peeping over your shoulder,
But may you sow them and Geige reap them,
And Morc garner them to the green barns![12]

Another waulking song satirizes the ex-lover who gave up his
girl when a wealthier catch came his way:

Last night I got not a wink of sleep,
Sorrow on me, sorrow on me!

This night I'll not get even as much,
Sorrow on me, sorrow on me!

Though she be tatty and freckly,
Her dusky cattle will make her stand out.

Though she be tatty and tousled,
Fat and fair are her Daddy's cattle.

Though she be wizened and wrinkly,
Fair and white are her Daddy's cattle.

Though she be skinny and like death,
O my love, what a hidden windfall!

Though her eyes be watery, sunken,
And her mouth an amber stone, she'll get a lover.

But I lie snug, longing for sleep,
Without cattle black or red or dappled.

Last night I got not a wink of sleep,
Sorrow on me, sorrow on me!

This night I'll not get even as much,
Sorrow on me, sorrow on me![13]

As in every age the pangs of love are often more remembered and more recorded than the delights and ecstasies. There are famous stories told and retold in the Gaelic about women who sacrificed their love for the sake of their lover, and bravely concealed their agony from inquisitive friends and neighbours and family. Catherine MacNeill told her story of self-sacrifice only when she was an old woman living in Barra and Carmichael went to visit her to hear her Gaelic lore. She was, he says, "poor and ailing, but full of charm, humour and wit, often at her own expense." She told her personal story in these words:

> My father and brother and myself and the man who was to marry me went away for a boat-load of seaweed. We over-loaded the boat and had to go by all the sheltered and shallow passages we could ... the boat took the ground, and my brother and my lover jumped out to lighten her. My father was preparing to follow them, but I could not bear to see my old father getting soaked, and I jumped out, though scolded by my father for my recklessness and teased by the young men for my bravery. I was up to my waist in water and remained wet till we got home at night. After that I became ill, and have continued more or less ill ever since ... The number of times the priests prayed me into the grave and the number of times they prayed me out of it![14]

Carmichael asked her had she never married after that, and she replied:

> No, my dear, I never married. Not at all because he was not eager to marry me, but I could not in honour marry, a poor cripple at death's door today, and on the hilltops tomorrow, down and up like the toss of the waves. I was not for depriving the fine lad of marriage and offspring — for that is what he was, a right good handsome noble lad and from a grand family. And I told him that since this nasty trouble took me, a shadow had come over my heart towards him and I could not marry him. May the eternal God of life forgive me for my lie! My heart was full and

like to break, but I was not for spoiling the fine lad, nor for depriving him of marriage and children.

Time and time again he came to see whether I would change my mind; but I said I was but a girl with one foot on the brink of the grave and the other foot in it, and it was but labour lost for him to strive with me. God forgive me, my heart was like to break!

The lad married a girl from the other side of the hill, a noble lass and from a fine family. That was the black day of sorrow, the black day of anguish for me, the day you married, Donald of the three Donalds, Donald son of Neill. 'Tis I can say and with truth:

> Without ease my heart was weeping,
> Though plain enough my smile.

I had no sleep at all for a week before or a week after it. Not a soul on earth knew how I was but my beloved mother, dearest of women.

The pangs of unrequited love could drive a woman to a crazed state, and one form this took was for the tormented woman to go off and wander with friendly animals, far from hurtful mankind. There are a number of variant tales on this theme of the woman who gives her heart to a faithless lover, who abandons her for a woman of wealth at the urging of his canny mother, but lives to regret his decision later on. She is called sometimes Flora of the Deer, and at other times the Melody Woman of the Hills, and this is one version of her story:

The melody woman of the hills

It is said that all creatures except man are partial to the insane and weak-minded. The maiden of the golden hair joined the deer in the mountains, travelling with them by day and sleeping with them at night. She became almost as fleet of foot as the deer themselves; the people of the country were pursuing her, but in vain. If at any time she seemed to falter or tire, the deer looked around and wistfully gazing at her awaited her coming.

The golden hair of the girl grew so long that it covered her like a cloak, while thick soft hair grew over her body like the soft fur of the spotted fawn, or like the soft fur of the spotted seal, and so nature, ever compassionate, enabled her to withstand the summer heat and the winter cold. With what food she sustained herself is not known, but it was supposed she lived on berries and nuts in season, and perhaps on hind's milk.

By degrees all the people in pursuit of the girl retired except her lover. He said he would go to the deer forest alone, but not alone return. After many days of wandering and many nights of sleeplessness the young man returned to his hiding cleft among the rocks; and there he found his golden-haired beloved lying sound asleep — white angels guarding her, my dear. Covering the beautiful form with the soft plaid from his own body, the young man waited and watched. When the girl opened her blue eyes and saw her lover, she addressed him by name and thanked him for the many kindnesses to her, not least the last.

"I am now going to die, Iain," she said, "and you will take me down to the townland and to the home of our childhood, and lay me to sleep beside my mother and among the dust of the kindred." And having sung this song for the ear of her lover she died in his arms.

And the young man put all the strength of his nature and all the energy of his manhood into himself and carried the girl's body to the homestead of the glen. After giving the story poem to others the young man laid himself down and died beside the girl. The two were buried side by side in the burial place of the green glen of their forebears, at the foot of the blue hills of the red grouse, the dun deer, the brown eagle and the white ptarmigan, and beside the clear stream of the silvery salmon that runs wailing and laughing and leaping day and night towards the heaving, mourning, everlasting sea. And from their two graves two weeping willows grew and twined around one another, stem and branch and bough. And the dusky thrush and the mottled mavis sang their morning elegies and their noonday mourning songs and their evening lullabies.[15]

This ancient tale of the folly of betraying true love, of friendly animals willing to help the human in sorrow, of reconciliation in the end, is found around the world in different versions. In the Highlands and Islands it took on new versions too, to make it more suitable to a Christian culture. The girl is portrayed singing of Christ's care and mercy to her during her ordeal in the wilderness, and the moral is to turn to the Lord, the only everpresent help in time of trouble.

> You great Lord of the sun,
> In the day of my need be near me,
> You great Being of the universe,
> Keep me in the sureness of your arms.
>
> Leave me not in dumbness,
> Dead in the wilderness,
> Leave me not to my stumbling,
> For my trust is in you, my Saviour.
>
> Though I had no fire,
> Your warmth did not fail me,
> Though I had no clothing,
> Your love did not leave me bare.
>
> Though I had no hearth,
> The cold did not numb me,
> Though I did not know the way,
> Your guidance was around me.
>
> Though I was in weakness,
> The hinds showed me kindness,
> Though I had no light,
> The night was as day.

Though I had no bed,
I was not missing sleep,
For Christ's arm was my pillow,
His eye excelling was my protecting.

Though I was neglected,
Hunger came not near me,
For Christ's body was my food,
The blood of Christ, it was my drink.

Though I had lost my reason,
You did not for a minute give me up,
Though I was out of my senses,
You did not choose to leave me.

Even if the stones were diamonds,
If they were coins of gold,
Even were the whole ocean wine
Gifted to me of right,

Even if the earth were cinnamon
And the lakes of honey —
Dearer to me would be a sight of Christ
In peace, in love, in pity.

Jesus, meet you my soul,
Jesus, clothe me in your charity,
Jesus, shield you my spirit,
Jesus, give me your hand.[16]

The consolations of religion

The coasts of the Highlands and Islands were dotted with *ceallan,* simple oratories built out of the natural rock, where travellers prayed to the God of the Elements before setting out on a sea crossing in the tempestuous waters of the Atlantic. In the fourteenth century the lady Amie set about building oratories

and nunneries and churches, after she had been cast off by her
husband, the Lord of the Isles, who wished for a new power pact
and took a new wife. He kept her extensive lands but she did
not give up, though defeated and deprived of her children and
her possessions. One of the oratories she built was St Michael's
on the isle of Grimsey in North Uist, and "in this little sanctuary
built for the purpose she offered prayers and thanks before and
after voyages to her kindred in Lorn."

The lady Amie took consolation for her lost earthly loves in
the household of heaven, where the Gaels imagined a kindly
Trinity of smiling affectionate love who would not let them down
as human loves often did:

> I am bending my knee
> In the eye of the Father who created me,
> In the eye of the Son who purchased me,
> In the eye of the Spirit who cleansed me,
> In friendship and affection.
> Through Thine own Anointed One, O God,
> Bestow upon us fullness in our need,
> Love towards God,
> The affection of God,
> The smile of God,
> The wisdom of God,
> The fear of God,
> And the will of God
> To do on the world of the Three,
> As angels and saints
> Do in heaven;
> Each shade and light,
> Each day and night,
> Each time in kindness,
> Give You us Your Spirit.[17]

3. Woman of mothering

Birth ceremonies

In the Western Isles the woman in labour went down on her right knee to give birth, so a woman would say of the number of children she had: I went three times upon my knee to my beloved Donald/John or whatever her spouse's name might be. In the old black houses the crofting women gave birth in the warmest place in the house, on a temporary bed of straw piled up in front of the fire. Neighbour women, and the township midwife if there was one, came to help at the birth, and they would always invoke the presence of St Brigid, because in their telling of the story of Christ's birth Brigid was Mary's "knee-woman" and became the baby's foster mother. In Celtic culture a foster mother was even dearer and closer than a blood mother, because she brought up the child, so Brigid won the name of being Mary of the Gael.

When the woman went into labour the midwife or one of the knee-women would go to the door of the house and beseech Brigid to be present at the birth, softly addressing Brigid and welcoming her in, while standing with open arms, one hand on each door jamb. If the birth goes well Brigid is present and friendly; if not, she is offended for some reason. Every birth, however ordinary, has a potential of being as extraordinary as the births in the Holy Family:

> There came to me assistance,
> Mary fair and Bride;
> As Anna bore Mary,
> As Mary bore Christ,
> As Eile bore John the Baptist

Without flaw in him,
Aid you me in my unbearing,
Aid me, O Bride.

As Christ was conceived of Mary,
Full perfect on every hand,
Help you me, foster-mother,
The conception to bring from the bone;
As you did aid the Virgin of Joy,
Without gold, without corn, without cattle,
Aid you me, for sore is my sickness,
Aid me, O Bride.[1]

Immediately after birth the baby was baptized by the midwife
or knee-woman, while the watching neighbour women joined
together in the singing that committed the newborn to the care
of the blessed Trinity. Catherine MacNeill of Barra described the
lay baptism of the knee-women in these words:

I heard this rune from old women in the long ago of the
world. When a child was born the midwife would put
three drops of water upon the forehead of the little one in
name of Father, in name of Son, in name of Spirit, and
she would say in this wise:

The little drop of the Father
On thy little forehead, beloved one.

The little drop of the Son
On thy little forehead, beloved one.

The little drop of the Spirit
On thy little forehead, beloved one.

To aid thee from the fays,
To guard thee from the host,

To aid thee from the gnome,
To shield thee from the spectre,

> To keep thee for the Three,
> To shield thee, to encompass thee,
>
> To save thee for the Three,
> To fill thee with the graces,
>
> The little drop of the Three
> To lave thee with the graces.[2]

The child was given a temporary name and blessing to last till the formal church baptism which usually happened eight days after birth, but there was no guarantee of that in the more remote islands where minister or priest might only visit once a year or less, and have to carry out a mass baptism of all the people born since his previous visit. The form of the lay baptism by the knee-women shows the relics of pre-Christian paganism in its litany of Otherworld figures who might snatch the child away and leave an ugly changeling in the cradle instead. The early Celtic church, it seems, was satisfied to overlay old religious ceremonies with new Christian forms, in order to win the ordinary people to the new faith. So at least until the nineteenth century the lay baptism of the kind described above was recognized by Presbyterian, Catholic and Anglican churches, and if the baby died before church baptism the burial could be in consecrated ground.

In explaining the need for the lay baptism Catherine MacNeill showed how much ordinary people had grafted new, that is, Christian, beliefs onto old. The watching women at the birth, she said, sing in witness of committing the baby to the Blessed Trinity, so that

> ... no seed of fairy, no seed of the hosts of the air, no seed
> of the world's people, can lift away the happy, tranquil
> little sleeper; eye [evil eye] cannot lie on him, malice
> cannot lie on him; the two arms of the mild Mary of grace
> and the two arms of gentle Christ are to free him, safe-
> guarding and surrounding and succouring the joyous
> little sleeper of the baptism.[3]

The first drop on the baby's forehead was to bequeath wisdom, the second drop was for peace, and the third drop was for purity.

Immediately after the knee-woman had completed the first baptism, she would hand the child to one of the aid-women for the first washing, and while she bathed the baby the women would sing the rune of the Nine Graces over him or her:

> A wavelet for thy form,
> A wavelet for thy voice,
> A wavelet for thy sweet speech,
>
> A wavelet for thy luck,
> A wavelet for thy good,
> A wavelet for thy health,
>
> A wavelet for thy throat,
> A wavelet for thy pluck,
> A wavelet for thy graciousness;
> Nine waves for thy graciousness.[4]

In other versions of the Rune of the Nine Graces the last verse takes the form of:

> The little palmful for thy eating,
> The little palmful for thy taking,
> The little palmful for thy vigour.[5]

And this is followed by a Christianizing end blessing:

> The little palmful of the Father,
> The little palmful of the Son,
> The little palmful of the Spirit.
>
> Nine little palmfuls of thy grace
> In the name of the Three in One.

Sometimes a gold or silver coin was put in the baby's first bath water, to bring a shower of blessings which are a blend of pagan and Christian wishes:

for love of peace, for love of means, for love of wealth,
for love of joyousness by day and by night,
for grace of goodness, for grace of fortune,
for grace of victory on every field.

In another of the many litanies of graces to bless a newborn
baby, we get a good idea of the things that were most longed for
and most admired in this Gaelic culture:

Litany of graces

Grace of form,
Grace of fortune,
Grace of voice,
Grace of Jesus Christ be ever thine,
Grace of the image of the Lord be thine.

Grace of men,
Grace of women,
Grace of lover,
Grace of sons and daughters be thine.

Grace of corn,
Grace of drink,
Grace of music,
Grace of guidance,
Grace of sea and land be thine.

Grace of sitting,
Grace of journeying,
Grace of cattle,
Grace of churning,
Grace of curds and butter be thine.

Grace of the duck of Mary [mallard],
Grace of the swan of the fountain,
Grace of sheep and of wool,
Grace of kids and of goats,
Enduring grace by day and by night be thine.

Grace of the love of the skies be thine,
Grace of the love of the stars be thine,
Grace of the love of the moon be thine,
Grace of the love of the sun be thine,
Grace of the love of the crown of heaven be thine.[6]

Invoking graces on a new baby was a very ancient practice, as is clear from fairy tales all around the world, where good and wicked fairies assemble to bring their blessings or their curses on the hapless infant. Traces of it are found even in the formal church baptism in the Western Isles. At the *fàeisd baistidh* or feast of baptism the baby was handed round from person to person in a sunwise direction, and everyone present was expected to make their own wish for the child. It was better if the wish was original and spontaneous, and that was often easier for people brought up in an oral culture, where readiness and wit of speech counted for something.

A baby who had not had any form of baptism, or a still born or aborted child, was thought to have no soul and therefore not to merit a burial on consecrated ground. But again the old pagan belief continued that even if such a child might lack a soul, it did have a spirit self and this spirit self, if given the proper burial in the right place, would make its home in a rock and become *mac talla,* child-of-rock, which in Gaelic means an echo. Unbaptized infants therefore were buried in a special remote place among rocks "between sundown and sunrise, without beam of sun or ray of moon, on a night black and dark, where no eye could see."

Birthing ceremonies were very much women's own, which they carried out without any male interference or even presence. They passed on the songs and traditional lore from mother to daughter, and had their own secret language for pregnancy and birth. Giving birth was "the sickness that gladdens every woman," or "the sighing of women, the solace of men." There were a number of herbs gathered from the local moorland and used in various ways to relieve the pains of childbirth. Artemisia or wormwood (in other countries used to make absinthe) with its sharp aromatic pungency was made into an infusion for drinking. *Am màothan,* which has been identified as probably the pearlwort or thyme-leaved sandwort (both members of the Pink family), was the most revered plant of all for protection against danger and illness and lack of love. A bunch of it was put underneath a woman in labour to ease her delivery, and sewn into the bodice during pregnancy as a safeguard against losing the baby.

The knee-woman or midwife had a high standing in her township, for on her fell the responsibility for bringing babies safely into the world. Catherine Pearson of Barra said:

> There was a midwife and a mourning-woman in every
> townland in Barra. And it was an obligation on the
> people of each townland to keep each woman of the kind
> in summer grass and winter fodder, to the satisfaction of
> the bailiff on the sword's edge. And the people would not
> see one of these suffer loss or want more than her
> neighbour, in order that each of them should be able to
> do her duty when it came to her, and alas for her who
> should not — she was the woman of the hard fate![7]

Brigid the aid-woman

The Christian saint Brigid continued many of the ways of the pagan goddess Brigid, who had presided over insight and augury, fertility, healing arts and crafts (and metalwork in particular). A sacred fire was kept burning in the women's enclosure at Kildare for many centuries after a Christian convent had replaced the old pagan sanctuary there. St Brigid's community of holy sisters took it in turns to nurture the sacred flame for nineteen nights, and on the twentieth night Brigid herself carried out the fire vigil. When the Welsh traveller Geraldus Cambrensis visited the monastic house at Kildare in the twelfth century, he reported that the nuns were still invoking Brigid every twentieth night with the plea, "Take care of your own fire, for this night is yours."

Brigid was neither missionary nor evangelist nor female martyr, like so many of the early Celtic saints. She appears rather as inspirer, protector and bringer of fertility to women, to crops, to livestock and to the artistic imagination. The stories told of her are a curious mixture of druidical wonderworking and Christian overlay. The pagan goddess of fire and fertility and spring is worked into the context of Scripture stories, as if to justify women's continuing affection for her, and make her acceptable to the Christian faith.

Typical of this process is the detailed account of how Brigid became aid-woman to Mary at the birth of Christ, and so divine midwife to every ordinary woman afterwards who invoked her help in giving birth. She is depicted as a serving maid at the inn in Bethlehem, and her master has given her stern instructions not to take in any more strangers, or give anyone food or drink, for there was a dearth in the land and he was guarding his resources prudently. But then, as the people of the Hebrides told the story of the Nativity, two strangers came up to the door of the inn:

> The man was old, with brown hair and grey beard, and
> the woman was young and beautiful, with oval face,
> straight nose, blue eyes, red lips, small ears, and golden
> brown hair which fell below her waist. They asked the
> serving-maid for a place to rest, for they were footsore
> and weary, for food to satisfy their hunger, and for water
> to quench their thirst. Bride could not give them shelter,
> but she gave them of her own bannock and of her own
> stoup of water, of which they partook at the door; and
> having thanked Bride the strangers went their way,
> while Bride gazed wistfully after them. She saw that the
> sickness of life was on the young woman of the lovely
> face, and her heart was sore that she had not the power
> to give them shade from the heat of the sun, and cover
> from the cold of the dew. When Bride returned into the
> house in the darkening of the twilight, what was stranger
> to her to see than that the bannock of bread was whole,
> and the stoup of water was full, as they had been before!
> She did not know under the land of the world what she
> would say or what she would do ...

When she recovered from her wonderment Bride went

out to look after the two who had gone their way, but she could see no more of them. But she saw a brilliant golden light over the stable door, and knowing that it was not a *dreag a bhais,* a meteor of death, she went into the stable and was in time to aid and minister to the Virgin Mother, and to receive the Child into her arms, for the strangers were Mary and Joseph, and the Child was Jesus Christ, the Son of God, come to earth, and born in the stable of the hostel of Bethlehem ...

When the Child was born, Bride put three drops of water from the spring of pure water [which had miraculously appeared], on the tablet of His forehead, in name of God, in name of Jesus, in name of Spirit.

When the master of the inn was returning home, and ascending the hill on which his house stood, he heard the murmuring of a stream flowing past his house, and he saw the light of a bright star above his stable door. He knew from these signs that the Messiah was come and that Christ was born — for it was in the seership of the people that Jesus Christ the Son of God would be born in Bethlehem, the town of David. And the man rejoiced with exceeding joy at the fulfilment of the prophecy, and he went to the stable and worshipped the new Christ, whose infant cradle was the manger of the horses.[8]

So Christ became the foster-child of Brigid, and she the midwife *par excellence,* and Bethlehem is peopled by Gaels and takes on the characteristics of the Gaelic lands. The story has all the elements of the synthesizing way of seeing the world that was especially Gaelic. They blended their own indigenous lore with the Christian Scriptures. They identified personally with the sufferings of the poor travellers Mary and Joseph, and responded as they were expected to do in their own hospitable culture — by adding the kindly compassionate Brigid to the New Testament story, because it was unthinkable that everyday warmth and aid were not forthcoming in the biblical account. The story of Brigid acting as midwife at the Birth of Births in turn shaped their own St Brigid Day celebrations on the first of February, for again they wove together past and present, history and myth, belief and action, true to their synthesizing ways. The young girls made a Brigid figure from a churn staff or a sheaf of corn and dressed her up with shining shells and crystals and snowdrops, putting on her breast a carefully woven Brigid's cross in memory of the star Brigid saw over the stable door the night she was aid-woman to Mary and helped bring Christ into the world. The girls then took their Brigid figure around the houses of the township, collecting bannocks and butter and cheese for a feast to which their young men were admitted to honour Brigid, for Brigid was much invoked by men as well as women, being still very much the goddess of fertility of sea and land and nature generally, as well as of female fertility.

Love children

Love children were called "lambs of the Lord" or "kirk chicks," since the church helped to contribute to their upkeep when their single mothers were struggling under the handicap of neighbours' disapproval and men's reluctance to marry "unrespectable" young women. A single mother was an affront to the conventions of a traditional community, for she was neither proper maid nor virtuous wife. "You bad black wench, you have sacrificed your snood and not justified your kertch," they said of such a one, referring to the distinctive change from hairband to three-cornered head kerchief on marriage. So single mothers sensitive to their families' and neighbours' disapproval sang laments like this:

> Tis the love child who has done for me,
> Tis the love child who has destroyed me,
> Tis the love child who has done for me,
> And the black smith of the torments.
>
> The black smith of catastrophes,
> The black smith of torments,
> Tis the black smith of catastrophes
> This day has wounded me.[9]

But the real feelings of the mother of a love child can be better read in the next lament, which is also a celebration of the baby. It points too at the harshness of some priests and ministers who refused baptism to love children, though the knee-women would still give the child a lay baptism. It is moving on the immediate and personal deprivations of a young single mother who can no longer go out freely and enjoy herself with the others in her group.

Lament for a love child

This is what leaves me joyless, that I have no baptism
        for you
Child of my love, 'twas you bore the heritage,
'Tis the unlucky coupling and your harsh father
Have left you so long a lamb of the Lord.

Here am I, sick when I see the lads off
In the young company of the girls,
Away to the dance house where the lot of them will
        have joy,
And me here at my fireside, alone.

Yet I'd not give you away, baby love, for a fortune,
Though I got all the gold of King George and his land.
I had rather yourself without cattle or treasure,
Though I bought you so dear with the bloom of
        my youth.[10]

There was a strong undertow of pagan fertility celebrations tugging against Christian marriage conventions, and a number of Christianized festivals seem to have encouraged lovemaking that might well bring babies of chance into the world. The most striking of these was the Michaelmas feast (see p. 60) at the end of summer, when in pagan times everything possible was done in the way of fertility rituals to ensure that as the year dipped down to sterility and cold and dark, there would be life and light born anew in the spring. Even after the feast had been adapted to Christianity and St Michael was its patron saint, many

ancient fertility celebrations remained, like the presentation by
the women of bunches of wild carrots to the men of their choice.
And the carrot, as Carmichael reminds us, is:

> a symbol of deep and high significance ... it symbolized
> fertility, offspring, children. The carrot was given by a
> woman to a man, rarely by a man to a woman. Girls and
> women were in the habit of gathering wild carrots on the
> sandy plains; when one gets a forked carrot she rejoices
> greatly, crying out in the fullness of her heart:

> > Dear little forked one! little forked one!
> > Carrot joy unstinting to me!
> > Dear little forked one! little forked one!
> > Carrot fulfilment unstinting to me!

> > Michael of the swords will give seed and fruit,
> > Brigid serene will give me passion,
> > Fite Fith [ravens?] will give me wine and milk,
> > And Mary mild will give me aid.[11]

A variant on the second verse gives a more open fertility
invocation:

> > Fruitfulness beyond fruitfulness,
> > Fruitfulness on my womb,
> > Fruitfulness beyond fruitfulness,
> > Fruitfulness on my own womb-fruit.

Home learning

In an oral culture learning is direct and personal, passed on in
house and field and on hill and loch through concrete experience.
Every aspect of daily life is part of the oral curriculum — work
and entertainment, past history and present joys or misfortunes,
dilemmas that have to be solved in a practical way, loves and

hates in a close-knit community that have to be worked out so that people can go on living in the same place. There is no end to this kind of direct learning, for it begins with the young child's seeing and copying what goes on around the place, and only ends with life itself, for the observation is continuous, of feast days and fast days and ordinary days, of birth and marriage and illness and death, of planting and harvesting, celebrating and mourning, laughing and crying and all the time hearing and telling stories about what's said and done by whom and when.

One of the old women on Barra who recited the lay baptism of the knee-woman to Carmichael, explained mother-to-daughter learning in these words:

> I heard this with my mother, peace to her soul, when I was but a poor tiny little urchin out and in at the threshold, as light and foolish as the birds of the air. O Mary Mother, little heed I gave these things at the time, and little did I think that you would come, dear one, to seek them today, after four score years. My dear mother was telling the ways of the townland to a woman from the hill land, and though I was small and foolish at the time, I was keeping an ear on her talk. And this is what my dear mother said to the woman who came to the house: When the child comes into the world, the knee-woman puts three drops of water on the forehead of the poor little infant, who has come home to us from the bosom of the everlasting Father. And the woman does this in the name and in the reverence of the kind and powerful Trinity, and says thus ...[12]

And the woman was able to recite the twenty-four lines of the lay baptism as she remembered them from her childhood. Clearly the oral culture trained people's memories to retain material and long after recite it at will, though different reciters would add their own variations and extemporize, for oral culture is not just rote learning, but develops and grows according to the imaginative energy of individuals and the degree of community support it has.

This Gaelic oral culture retained something of a medieval way of seeing the world, which post-Renaissance thinking tends to undervalue, if not deride. There was a strong conviction that everything that existed in this world or the Otherworld was part of a whole, was interconnected, so that if you could only see the connections you would understand whatever is. New discoveries or new happenings would be examined for their similarity or difference to what was already known, in order to fit them into the scheme of things. There might be, here and there, eccentric folk called experts or specialists, but they had lost the fullness of their humanity usually by becoming experts, and lived in a rarefied stratosphere which left ordinary people free to go on speculating on the meaning of things, factually and fictionally (for the dividing line was by no means clear in getting at the truth — storytelling was the thing).

The children got a lot of their education by listening to the grown-ups till the late hour of the family going to bed, for in the crowded black houses there were no distant bedrooms where children slept. Even if they were put to bed in some partitioned-off corner or loft, they would be able to hear every word of the grown-ups through the thin boards:

> I remember myself, though I was but little at the time,
> when the Christian folk crowded into one another's
> houses, telling tales and histories, invocations and
> prayers, singing hymns and songs, runes and lays, sweet,
> beautiful and soft ... The old people conversed about the
> state of the world and about the changes of the weather,
> about the moon and the sun, about the stars of the sky,
> about the ebbing and flowing of the sea, about the life in
> the depths of the ocean, and about the hot and cold lands
> of the earth. We children would be sitting on the bare flat
> of the floor, not uttering a syllable, not moving a hand,
> lest we should be put out of the house if we were not
> mannerly. O King, 'tis there would be the talk — and
> noble talk![13]

As well as absorbing the grown-ups' songs and story-telling, the children would be taught specific celebratory prayers and blessings by their own mothers, to be said on the everyday occasions of rising in the morning, getting dressed, mealtimes, and going to bed. In this category falls the night prayer that follows, from a woman who knew innumerable songs and chants from her own parents and who had passed them on to her own children who were now themselves dead. She said she still thought over those old hymns and songs that she had heard in her childhood and never since, for they were very different and very weird and very beautiful:

Night shielding

My God and my Chief,
I seek to You in the morning,
My God and my Chief,
I seek to You this night.
I am giving You my mind,
I am giving You my will,
I am giving you my wish,
My own soul eternal and my own body.

Be You chieftain over me,
Be You my laird to me,
Be You my shepherd over me,
Be You my guardian unto me,
Be You my herdsman over me,
Be You my guide to me,
Be you with me, O Chief of Chiefs,
Father everlasting and God of the heavens.[14]

Catherine Maclennan of Moidart remembered her mother's teaching and rearing with precise vividness:

My mother was always at work, by day helping my father on the croft, and by night at the wool and the spinning, for night clothes and for day clothes for the family. My mother would be beseeching us to be careful in everything, to put value on time and to avoid idleness; for that a night was coming in which no work could be done. She would be warning us about MacShiamain [a user even of straw, thus a Busy Man] and how he sought to be at work. If we were dilatory about putting on our clothes, and made an excuse for our prayers, my mother would say that God regarded heart and not speech, the mind and not the manner ... She would be asking us to sing our morning song to God down in the back-house, as Mary's lark was singing it up in the clouds, and as Christ's mavis was singing it yonder in the tree, giving glory to the God of the creatures for the repose of the night, for the light of the day, and for the joy of life. She would tell us that every creature on the earth here below and in the ocean beneath and in the air above was giving glory to the great God of the creatures and the worlds, of the virtues and the blessings, and would *we* be dumb?[15]

So mothers passed on to their children a way of feeling as well as a way of doing. Their daughters while they learned the skills of the woman of the house (the churning, the hatching, the spinning and weaving) also learned a whole repertoire of songs and blessings for each of these tasks. There was a song for going to fetch water from the well after dark (in case the bogeys were waiting). There were the baking blessings and rituals so that the family and guests might share in simple but truly sacramental meals. There were the healing runes to chant while applying herbal remedies. It was as if the doing of something was not enough on its own; there had to be imagination and self-expression to go with the doing. You might call this, I suppose, the feeling intelligence, or the affective action. Whatever you call it, it embodies a way of living that seeks to give the most ordinary experiences meaning, and to bring back into a whole the mind, emotion and spirit that our more sophisticated culture chops apart.

The blessings and ceremonies that mothers organized when their children departed from home are a good example of this way of combining practical action with personal feeling. When a child left for the mainland, as they often did (and still have to) to find work and explore the wider world, family and friends gathered in the house to bless the departing one with kind words and a home-made gift of a plaid or stockings or gloves they had knitted themselves. Sometimes the pilgrim setting out (for that was the word often used, as of a quest or discovery journey), would bathe the face in warm ewe's milk, in memory of Mary bathing the infant Christ in blessed milk on the flight into Egypt, and would sing the *Duil Deora*, Pilgrim's Hope:

> I will bathe my face
> In the nine rays of the sun,
> As Mary washed her Son
> In the milk of the generous deer.
>
> Mildness be on my lips,
> Kindness be on my face,
> Chasteness be on my desire,
> Wisdom be in my purpose.
>
> The love that Mary gave to her one Son
> May the whole world give me;
> The love that Jesus gave to John the Baptist
> May I give to all who meet me.
>
> Be the Son of God at the outset of my journey,
> Be the Son of God sure to aid me,
> Be the Son of God making clear my way,
> Be the Son of God at the end of my seeking.[16]

The departure of a child was particularly poignant for the mother, since it was well known that she might never set eyes on the child again, once they went out into the wide world, and the daughter or son who did come home for visits might be so changed that perpetual estrangement might follow from want of words to bridge the gap. Catherine MacPhee of Uist did not like what she saw of the Island daughters who returned like turn-of-the-century yuppies:

> The young women of today have neither bone nor body, nor the growth proper to women. If they make a trip to

the lowlands they come back home stuffed with airs and pride, and who but they? They go to Mass and to church to show themselves off, and who but they? With a knot on their breast and a fancy dress on their back, a picture hat on their head and a sunshade in their hand held above their head, and Mary Mother! who but they? — looking down on the mothers that bore them, because they had nothing of that sort and it did not even exist in their time! May God give them sense! It is themselves would need that, and who would need to go to the knoll to see if the fairy woman would bestow the wisdom and grace of womanhood on them.[17]

Whatever their worries about their departing children, and their own personal grieving over their loss, the mothers put a brave face on it and sent the child off with a personal blessing:

> The joy of God be in your face,
> Joy to all who see you,
> The arms of God around your neck,
> Angels of God shielding you,
> Angels of God shielding you.
>
> Joy of night and day be yours,
> Joy of sun and moon be yours,
> Joy of men and women be yours,
> Each land and sea you go on,
> Each land and sea you go on.
>
> Be every season happy for you,
> Be every season bright for you,
> Be every season glad for you,
> And the Son of Mary Mother at peace with you,
> And the Son of Mary Mother at peace with you.
>
> Be yours the compassing of the God of Life,
> Be yours the compassing of the Christ of Love,
> Be yours the compassing of the Spirit of grace
> To befriend you and support you

> *Catherine / Donald* [the child is named here in person]
> You dear one of my heart.[18]

Finally all present at the farewell for the departing child would join in a slow and solemn singing of the parting hymn:

> Be the Great God between your two shoulders,
> To protect you in your going and in your coming,
> Be the Son of Mary Mother near your heart,
> And be the perfect Spirit upon you pouring —
> Oh, the perfect Spirit upon you pouring.[19]

Mary and the mothering of compassion

The Russian mystic Paul Evdokimov says in *La femme et le salut du monde* that "even spiritual fatherhood employs images of motherhood: *I am in labour pains until Christ be formed in you (Galatians 4:19)."* He suggests that "the most amazing thing we have still to discover is the fact that man does not possess the paternal instinct to the same degree and intensity that woman possesses the maternal instinct." Spiritual mothering needs to be done by both women and men, for it is the way we express our solidarity with other human beings and our solidarity with the rest of creation. If mothering is confined to the domestic and private the whole cosmos suffers. Mary therefore is being given a new focal place in Christianity by liberation theologians, because in her mothering becomes universal rather than particular, and yet she is Everywoman, struggling with the ordinary everyday things that women go on doing in all times and places.

In the Western Isles there was great personal affection and respect for the divine mother Mary, because although she was the Mother of God and the model of divine compassion, she remained "one of us," and so was like a close woman friend who could be called upon in any crisis for practical help and support. The word *Moire* for Mary was kept only for the Blessed Virgin, and was often used in talk by both Catholic and Protestant

women, as in "Be still, children, be quiet now, you would cause
the mild Mary of grace even to lose her temper." Although Brigid
was called the Mary of the Gaels, the Celtic social system made
it possible for Brigid and Mary both to do the mothering of
Christ — Mary as blood mother and Brigid as foster mother (see
p. 80). Indeed they were considered to be great friends, sharing
in bringing up the baby Jesus, consoling each other when he
started going off on his strange adventures, and using Gaelic
divination to find him when he would not say where he was
going or what he was up to. The closeness of the two women
continued even after Jesus was a grown man. Brigid's husband,
they said, brought Jesus the water to wash the feet of his
disciples.

As was the habit in the Gaelic oral culture, the Scripture
stories were retold to incorporate favourite Gaelic saints;
they were relocated to their own beloved crofting landscapes,
and they were given everyday details that made them immediately recognizable and relevant to the ordinary life of
their own communities. So when Mary is pregnant with the
Son of God, she still suffers from the irrational hunger for
some particular food, like ordinary women do, and Joseph is
portrayed as an ordinary husband needing to be convinced that
this divine pregnancy is not just an excuse for her faithlessness
to him:

Christ's first miracle

Joseph and Mary were on their way
To the taking of the census,
And the birds began chorusing
In the dove-dwelling woods.

The two were walking the track,
Till they came to a deep thicket,
And in the thicket was fruit
That was red as the raspberry.

That was the time she was big,
That she was carrying the King of grace,

And she took a desire for the fruit
That was growing on the breast of the hill.

Then spoke Mary to Joseph
In a tone low and sweet,
"Give to me of the fruit, Joseph,
For me to quench my desire."

Then spoke Joseph to Mary,
And the hard pain in his heart,
"I will give you of the fruit, Mary,
But tell me the father of your burden?"

Then it was that the baby spoke up
From the inside of her womb,
"Bend you down every beautiful branch,
Till my mother may satisfy her want."

And from the branch that was highest
To the branch that was lowest,
They all bowed down to her knee,
And Mary tasted the fruit
In her beloved land of promise.

Then Joseph said to Mary,
And he heavy with remorse,
"It is carrying Him you are,
The King of glory and grace.
Blessed be you, Mary,
Among the women of all lands.
Blessed be you, Mary,
Among the women of all lands."[20]

When Jesus as a boy goes off to argue with the rabbis in the temple, Mary and Brigid follow the Gaelic practice of using the second sight to locate him. Mary (and sometimes Brigid too) makes her hand into a seeing tube and conjures the picture of the missing boy:

Mary's augury

The augury Mary mild made for her Son,
Was the gazing downward through her palm;
"Did you get a glimpse of the King of Life?"
The fair Queen said that she saw.

"I see Christ of the curly hair,
In the Temple of the King of hosts,
Arguing there with the frowning professors,
A while before they closed their court."[21]

Mary filled the old role of mother goddess of fertility, as she did
in many other parts of the Christian world (the Madonna of the
Pomegranate in southern Italy absorbed the ancient veneration
of the goddess Hera Argiva, holding Christ on one arm instead
of her son-lover, and her pomegranate in her other hand). The
Gaels blended pagan and Christian elements without any
agonizing among the ordinary people about doctrinal correctness.
So we find prayers to Mary for the blessing of the land and the
crops:

O Mary Mother of wondrous power,
Grant us the succour of your strength,
Bless the provisioning, bless the board,
Bless the ear, the corn, the food.

The Virgin of glowing presence,
The Jesus more bright-white than snow,
She like the moon in the crests arising,
He like the sun on the mountain heights.[22]

Her feast day on August 15 continued ancient ceremonies for
ensuring fertility in the coming year. A special bannock was
baked from the new corn, and shared among the household. The
animals too were collected in for their Mary blessing, and the
whole household went processing round the circuit of steading
and fields as a way of encompassing them within Mary's
protection and fruitfulness for another season.

There are beautiful litanies emphasising Mary's universal mothering — her role as mother of the cosmos does not give her the remoteness that the all-powerful Father God sometimes connotes, for she still remains the good mother, close and compassionate:

> Since you are the star of ocean,
> Pilot me at sea.
> Since you are the star of earth,
> Guide me on land.
>
> Since you are the star of night,
> Lighten me in the darkness.
> Since you are the sun of day,
> Encompass me on land.
>
> Since you are the star of angels,
> Watch over me on earth.
> Since you are the star of paradise,
> Companion me to heaven.
>
> Be you my safeguarding by night,
> Be you my safeguarding by day,
> Be you my safeguarding both day and night,
> You bright and kindly queen of heaven.[23]

Mary in the Gaelic culture was a model for a very practical kind of compassion, such as everyday mothers practised with their earthly children. This often took the form of healing, since mothers usually take charge when sickness and injury threaten the household, and patiently do the caring till the patient is better. In this final way of seeing Mary, even Jesus the Great Healer acknowledges his Mother's healing powers and defers to her, presumably because in the day-to-day experiences of the Gaels it was the mothers you turned to in sickness and stress. (Note that the Holy Land is now a Scottish glen).

> Jesus and his mother were walking by the side of a river
> in the Holy Land. And what was it but a gentle Autumn

evening, the sun about to sink in the depths of the ocean,
scattering gold-yellow and gold-red upon the crests of the
mountains and upon the surface of the waves. And in the
meeting of day and night, what but a white-bellied
salmon leaped with a great plunge up the rough bed of
the stream. Christ saw that the salmon was wanting the
sight of an eye, and he desired the Mary Mother to give
the sight of the eye back to the salmon. And the Mary
Mother gave the sight of that eye back to the salmon, and
the sight of that eye was every bit as good as that of the
other eye.[24]

The salmon is the symbol of wisdom in pagan Celtic mythology,
and in this story it is found half blind and in need of healing. It
is the Christian Mary Mother who heals the wisdom salmon,
while the Son of God urges her on to use her miraculous healing
powers. It is an intriguing blend of pagan and Christian myth,
where Christ the Logos of the New Testament acknowledges the
ancient wisdom — the mothering of compassion.

4. Woman of the seasons

Sun, moon and the elements

The women of the Western Isles lived close to the natural elements and their lives were marked by the turning of the seasons, made visible by the phases of the moon and the wheeling of summer and winter sun high or low in the sky above them. They had runes for singing to sun and moon and stars, to thunder and lightning, to wind and water. No doubt there was a pre-Christian heritage to this vivid awareness of the natural environment, for their pagan predecessors had peopled nature with benign or malign spirits — in every river and crag, wood and knoll, bog and waterfall. But there was no difficulty adapting it to Christianity for Genesis outlined the story of God creating the universe, and it was all good and worthy of reverence. And there are parallels in other branches of Christianity, most strikingly in the tradition of St Francis who speaks of Brother Sun and Sister Moon, respecting the wholeness of the creation. Mor MacNeill of Barra, an old woman who lived on her own in the poorest of material circumstances, explained the Gaelic view of the elements:

> In the time of my father and mother there was no man in Barra who would not take off his bonnet to the white sun of power, nor a woman in Barra who would not bend her body to the white moon of the seasons. No, my dear, not a man or woman in Barra. And old persons will be doing this still, and I will be doing it myself sometimes. Children mock at me, but if they do, what of that? Is it not much fitter for me to bend my body to the sun and to the moon and to the stars, that the Great God of life made for my good, than to the son or daughter of earth like myself?[1]

Sun greetings

On getting up in the morning people greeted the sun as soon as
it appeared over the crest of the hills, and they greeted it again
in the evening as it sank down into the western ocean, often in
fiery splendour. From the isle of Barra off South Uist comes this
hymn to the morning sun.

> Hail to you, you sun of the seasons,
> As you traverse the lofty skies,
> Your way is strong on the wing of the heavens,
> You are the glowing mother of the stars.
>> You have your lying down in the destroying ocean
>> Without harming, without fear;
>> You rise on the serene hill crest
>> Like a queenly woman in bloom.[2]

The rising and setting of the sun was a symbol of the hope of
resurrection, as this prayer from Arisaig shows:

> I am in hope, in the proper time,
> That the great and kindly God
> Will not put out for me the light of grace,
> Like you are leaving me this night.[3]

But it also stood for the life force which reached its perfection in
the God of life, as a hymn to the sun from Barra and South Uist
pictures it:

> The eye of the great God,
> The eye of the God of glory,
> The eye of the King of hosts,
> The eye of the King of the living,
> Pouring down on us
> At every time and season,
> Pouring down on us
> At every time and season.
>> Glory to you, you sun of glory,
>> Glory to you, you face of the God of life.[4]

On Easter Sunday the sun dances in joy for the risen Lord, said
Barbara Macphie of Dreimsdale:

> The glorious gold-bright sun was after rising on the crests
> of the great hills, and it was changing colour — green,
> purple, red, blood-red, white, whitest white and gold-
> white, like the glory of the God of the elements to the
> children of humanity. It was dancing up and down
> exulting at the joyous resurrection of the beloved Saviour
> of victory.[5]

To be blessed with a sight of the sun dances on Easter Day, she
said, a person had to climb to the top of the highest hill before
sunrise, and believe in her heart that "the God who makes the
small blade of grass to grow is the same God who makes the
great massive sun to move."

Christ's birth was seen too as the coming of a great light to
benighted earth, to spread warmth and vibrant life where before
there was coldness and darkness and no shape on anything.

> A time ere came the Son of God,
> The earth was a black bog
> Without star, without sun, without moon,
> Without body, without heat, without form.
>
> Illumined plains, illumined hills,
> Illumined the great green sea,
> Illumined the whole globe altogether,
> When the Son of God came to earth.[6]

In the Western Isles there is a far greater consciousness of different kinds of light, for the next wave of weather can usually be
seen moving in over the Atlantic and swathing one range of hills
in watery mist, while the neighbour hills are bathed in sunlight.
Sea and sky change colour constantly and you can see a dozen
rainbows on the same afternoon arched between sea and land.
The Gaelic language reflects this play of the elements in its rich
vocabulary for different kinds of light, in a parallel way to the
celebration of sunlight and moonlight, starlight and fire in the

hymns and prayers. Alexander Carmichael explains the meaning of the untranslateable *teine tana* light in these terms: "Thin light, evanescent light, phosphorescent, fitfully flitting over the mane of a horse on a calm drizzly night." As he drove across the fords and along the machairs of the Outer Hebrides to talk to the people and listen to their lore, he would often notice this fitful light on the mane of his horse, or shining on the backs of the grazing cattle, and found there were a number of vivid names for it, including "wolf's light" and "the fire of the russet dog," that is fox-fire or deceptive fire.

It is no wonder then that there is a wealth of hymns and prayers to sun and moon and stars, and that the elements of air and light loom large in the other poems too, as in this celebration of the famed horse of St Michael, Brian or Brianag (St Michael being patron saint of horses as well as dragon slayer and inheritor of a sun god tradition in which his chariot swept across the sky):

St Michael's steed

Michael's Brian was
As white as the snow of the peaks,
As white as the foam of the waves,
As white as the cotton of the moorland,
And nearly as white as the angel victorious.

Michael's Brian was
As swift as the swallow of the spring,
As swift as the winds of march,
As swift as the bolt of lightning,
And nearly as swift as the shaft of death.[7]

Moon greetings

The sun was an orb of fiery power and awe, but the moon was seen rather as "a friend of great love, guiding their course upon land and sea, and their path wherever they went." Though the sun is sometimes seen as female (as in *Hail to the sun,* p. 98), it was more often associated with the male, and the moon with the female.

The moon was known to affect growth and development of multiple kinds, from the ebbing and flowing of the tides to the cycle of women's menstruation. So a whole set of beliefs grew up about the right time in the moon's cycle to carry out various activities. In the waning of the moon it was bad to kill pig or sheep or other animal, because the meat would be "without taste, without sap, without plumpness, without fat." Similarly it was the wrong time to cut pine for a boat, or willow for baskets or creels, for the sap would be down and the wood brittle in the dark wane of the moon.

New moon was therefore the right time to start important tasks like reaping the crops, shearing the sheep, or cutting the peats. And it was a matter of spiritual courtesy to greet the new moon by hailing her first appearance and by turning over the lucky penny three times in the pocket, to safeguard luck during this new moon's cycle. Some of the moon prayers are closer than others to pagan moon worship, in that they exclude any reference to the Trinity or the Christian saints:

Hail to the new moon

Hail to you, you new moon,
Guiding gem of gentleness!
I am bending to you my knee,
I am offering to you my love.

I am bending to you my knee,
I am giving you my hand,
I am lifting to you my eye,
O new moon of the seasons.

Hail to you, you new moon,
Joyful maiden of my love!
Hail to you, you new moon,
Joyful maiden of the graces!

You are journeying in your course,
You are steering the full tides,
You are illumining to us your face,
O new moon of the seasons.

You queen-maiden of guidance,
You queen-maiden of good fortune,
You queen-maiden, my dear one,
You new moon of the seasons.[8]

But more often the moon greetings are infused with Christian spirit, the moon being seen as a blessed part of God's creation, and all who look on her are reminded that they are part of that same creation. Each moon cycle is a reminder also that we are a step nearer our own "crossing of the black river of death," and should be mindful of our own lives as part of the natural cycles of waxing and waning to which all created things are subject. That is not a matter of sorrow but of acceptance of the cyclical view of the passing of time that the moon teaches us.

A Hymn to the New Moon was sung by the people of South Uist at the summer shielings, where there would be a gathering of women and girls mainly, with a few men and boys out from the township for the evening, and they might be, as in Alexander Carmichael's idyll:

> ... singing and dancing, carolling and prancing, upon the green grass under the shining light of the moon, the moonbeams shimmering upon the clear lake below, while the fleecy clouds moved slowly above, showing the blue, beautiful sky in the far-away distance, with the projecting rocks and the heath-clad everlasting hills at hand. The "Hooching" of the men, the clapping of the girls, the mouth-music of the women, and the reverberations in the rocks combined with the surroundings to make up a picture that can neither be described nor forgotten.[9]

New moon

There she is, the new moon,
The King of life blessing her;
Fragrant be every night
That she shall shine on!

Be her lustre full
To each one in need,
Be her course complete
To each one in trouble.

Be her light above
With every one in straits,
Be her light below
With every one in want.

May the moon of moons
Be coming through thick clouds
On me and every other
Coming through dark tears.

May God's hand on me stay
In every strait that on me strays,
Now and till the hour of my death,
And till my resurrection day.[10]

Another rune for reverencing the new moon draws out the
oneness of all creation, and was recited while bowing down to
the moon and making the sign of the cross "over the tablet of the
heart":

Be your light fair to me!
Be your course smooth to me!
If luck to me is your beginning,
Seven times more be your ending,
You white moon of the seasons,
You great gleaming of grace!

He who created you
Created me too;
He who gave you shape and shining
Gave me life and death,
And the joy of the seven happinesses,
You great gleaming of grace,
You white moon of the seasons.[11]

Festivals of the seasons

The four turning points in the Gaelic year were St Brigid's day, February 1, marking the beginning of spring, the return of light and growth to the dead land; Beltane or May Day at the beginning of summer; Lugnasa or Lammas, the time of harvesting and matchmaking; and Samhain or All Hallows (our Halloween) on October 31, marking the coming of winter. On these four quarter days rents and debts were paid, farming help hired, and stocktaking done. They were occasions for pausing and considering the future, for completing schemes and working out new schemes. Auguries were made for the coming quarter to find out what were the favourable times and the ill-starred times for new ventures such as marriage or building a new house or going on a journey.

Christian feast days were fitted in alongside the old festivals of the seasons — Michaelmas on September 29, Mary's Feast on August 15, and of course Christmas at the time of the old winter solstice, when the year turned and light began to come back with hopes of renewal. On the basis of the surviving songs and prayers in the *Carmina Gadelica*, the favourite festivals of the Gaels were the feasts of their beloved saints Brigid, Columba, Mary and Michael, together with Beltane (May Day) and Christmas or Hogmanay.

Brigid's feast

Brigid with her white wand was said to breathe life and warmth into the dead winter, to make him open his eyes to the returning life of spring, with its tears of showers and laughter of bluster-ing winds.[12]

> Bride dipped her finger in the river
> On the Feast Day of Bride,
> And away went the hatching mother of the cold;
> She washed the palms of her hands in the river
> On the Feast Day of Patrick,
> And away went the conceiving mother of the cold.

On this first day of spring, with light returning and signs of growth beginning again, there was a special service in the churches, where the priest reminded his listeners:

> ... that the great God who made the land and all thereon,
> also made the sea and all therein, and that the wealth of
> sea and the plenty of land, the treasury of Columba and
> the treasury of Mary, are His gift to them that follow
> Him and call upon His name on rocky hill or on crested
> wave. The priest urges upon them to avoid disputes and
> quarrels over their fishing, to remember the dangers of
> the deep and the precariousness of life, and in their fish-
> ing to remember the poor, the widow and the orphan, now
> left to the fatherhood of God and to the care of His people.

This was on some of the islands a preliminary to drawing lots for the fishing banks, and to counting the flocks, and putting the renewed cycle of activities under the protection of St Brigid, for she was held to preside over the seasons, assigning to each their own proper activities.

There were special ceremonies by which the girls and women appealed to Brigid for her guidance and support in the new cycle of the seasons. While the young girls made an image of Brigid, beautifully dressed and decorated, to carry round the houses collecting for their own feast of hospitality to the boys, the older women made a Brigid's bed and put on it an ikon of Brigid made of a sheaf of corn and covered with handwoven ribbons and spring flowers from the hillside. As Carmichael describes the scene in one of the townships on St Brigid's Eve:

> One woman goes to the door of the house, and standing
> on the step with her hands on the jambs, calls softly into

the darkness, *"Tha leaba Bride deiseal,"* "Bride's bed is
ready." To this a ready woman behind replies, *"Thigeadh
Bride steach, is e beatha Bride,"* "Let Bride come in, Bride
is welcome." The woman at the door again addresses
Bride ... "Bride, come you in, your bed is ready. Preserve
the house for the Trinity." The women then place the
ikon of Bride with great ceremony in the bed ... They
place a small straight white wand (the bark being peeled
off) beside the figure ... of birch, broom, bramble, white
willow or other sacred wood, crossed or banned wood
being carefully avoided. A similar rod was given to the
kings of Ireland at their coronation, and to the Lords of
the Isles at their instatement. It was straight to typify
justice, and white to signify peace and purity — blood-
shed was not to be needlessly caused. The women then
level the ashes on the hearth, smoothing and dusting
them over carefully ... In the early morning the family
closely scan the ashes. If they find the marks of the wand
of Bride they rejoice, but if they find the footprint of
Bride, their joy is very great, for this is a sign that Bride
was present with them during the night, and is favourable to them, and that there is an increase in family,
flock, and in field during the coming year. Should there
be no marks on the ashes, and no traces of Bride's
presence, the family are dejected. It is to them a sign that
she is offended, and will not hear their call. To propitiate
her and gain her ear the family offer oblations and burn
incense. The oblation generally is a cockerel, some say a
pullet, buried alive near the junction of three streams,
and the incense is burnt on the hearth when the family
retire for the night.

There were other pagan remnants in the Brigid Day celebrations. "The serpent emerged from its hole" and a propitiatory
hymn was sung to it, with some very ambivalent ritual acts, as
if at one time the serpent had been venerated, before it became
accursed with the coming of the Christian faith where the
serpent was to blame for the fall from paradise.

Early on Brigid's morning
The serpent shall come from the hole;
I will not molest the serpent,
Nor will the serpent molest me.

The serpent was in some variations of the hymn called the queen, and may at one time have symbolized the unified sexual or life forces of male and female which combined to generate new life. But in its final form, the ritual was a condemnation of the serpent presumably as symbol of carnal lust, greed or devious cunning. A piece of peat was put in a stocking and pounded with a stick to enact the crushing of the serpent's head.

There were many versions of the Genealogy of Brigid, too, which equally show a blend of pagan and Christian forms of protection and supplication. Genealogies were learnt by heart in the Celtic lands and were of prime importance in establishing one's *bona fide* belongingness, since if people knew who you were they could trust you, or if you broke their trust, could go to your family to demand compensation. So to recite the genealogy of Brigid was to establish her credentials not only as a Christian saint but as a descendant of an Irish royal house with an obligation to protect and aid their people in times of trouble.

The genealogy of Brigid

Brigid daughter of Dugall the Brown,
Son of Aodh, son of Art, son of Conn,
Son of Criara, son of Cairbre, son of Cas,
Son of Cormac, son of Cartach, son of Conn.

Brigid of the mantles,
Brigid of the peat-heap,
Brigid of the twining hair,
Brigid of the augury.

Brigid of the white feet,
Brigid of serenity,
Brigid of the white palms,
Brigid of the kine.

Brigid, companion-woman,
Brigid of the peat-heap,
Brigid, aid to women,
Brigid, woman kindly.

Brigid, own tress of Mary,
Brigid, nurse of Christ,
Each day and each night
That I say the genealogy of Brigid,

I shall not be slain,
I shall not be wounded,
I shall not be prisoned,
I shall not be gashed,
I shall not be torn in sunder,
I shall not be plundered,
I shall not be down-trodden,
I shall not be stripped,
I shall not be rent in two,
Nor will Christ let me be forgotten.

Nor sun shall burn me,
Nor fire shall burn me,
Nor beam shall burn me,
Nor moon shall burn me.

Nor river shall drown me,
Nor salt-water drown me,
Nor flood drown me,
Nor water drown me.

Nightmare shall not lie on me,
Black-sleep shall not lie on me,
Spell-sleep shall not lie on me,
Sleep-sickness shall not lie on me.

I am under the keeping
Of my Saint Mary;
My companion dear to me
Is Brigid.[13]

The feast of Beltane (May Day)

This was the purification and renewal festival to bring protection and blessing on the growing crops and young animals, as well as increase on the fortunes of people and house. The hearth fires were renewed from a communal *tein eigin* or need fire, the animals were driven between the two flaming heaps of the *tein eigin,* and the Beltane blessing was sung.

Beltane blessing

Bless, You Threefold true and generous,
Myself, my spouse, and my little ones,
My tender children and their beloved mother at
        their head,
On the fragrant plain, on the happy mountain shieling,
On the fragrant plain, on the happy mountain shieling.

All in my household and in my possessing,
All cows and crops, all flocks and corn,
From Hallow Eve to Beltane Eve
With burgeoning and kindly benefit.
From sea to sea, and every river mouth,
From wave to wave, and depths of waterfall.

Be the Three Persons taking possession of all in
        my belonging,
Be the trusted Trinity keep me in truth;
O nourish my soul with the talk of Paul,
And safeguard my dear ones beneath the wing of
        your glory,
Safeguard my dear ones beneath the wing of
        your glory.

Bless everything and everyone
Of this household here with me,
Put the Christ cross on us with a power of love,
Till we see the land of joy,
Till we see the land of joy.

The time the cattle shall go out of the stalls,
The time the sheep shall go out of the folds,
The time the goats go up to the misty mountain,
Be the care of the Trinity following them,
Be the care of the Trinity following them.

You Being who created me at the beginning,
Listen to me and be here as I go down on my knees
        to You,
Each morning and each evening, and I mindful
In Your own company, God of life,
In Your own company, O God of life.[14]

There were many Beltane blessings in the same spirit, but
dedicated to the favourite Mary Mother, as well as to the
Trinity.

The Mary blessing on Beltane

Mary, you mother of blessed ones,
Bless our flocks and mother cows,
Hate and harm keep you away,
Drive off from us the bad doers.

Keep your eye every Monday and Tuesday
On the mothering kine and the pairing beasts;
Come you with us from hill to shore,
You gather the sheep and their lambs.

Every Wednesday and Thursday be with them,
Be your kindly hand always about them,
Tend the cows down to their stalls,
Tend the sheep down to their folds.

Every Friday be you, Saint, at their head,
Lead the sheep from the face of the bens,
With their innocent little lambs after them,
Encompass them with God's enfolding.

> Every Saturday be with them the same,
> Bring the goats in with their young,
> Every kid and nanny to the shore side,
> Down from the Rock of Aegir up on the heights,
> With the green cresses round its summit ...[15]

Beltane, like the other festivals of the seasons, was marked by a family feast, for which the women did a special baking of cakes and the shieling feast (for Beltane was the day of the move to the mountain pastures) would include a "male lamb, without spot or blemish, killed that day. Formerly this lamb was sacrificed, now it is eaten. The feast is shared with friends and neighbours; all wish each other luck and prosperity, with increase in their flocks." After the feasting the shepherding of the Old Testament forefathers (Abraham and Isaac and Jacob) was invoked and the shepherding of God Himself on the Protestant parts of the Western Isles, while the Catholics added their appeals to Michael and Columba and Brigid and Mary.

The feast of St Michael

> And the night of St Michael's Feast! That was the
> delightful night in Uist! A ball and dancing, beer and
> feastfare by every doorpost. And the young girls' hidden
> stores, and no knowing under the sun when or where
> they had got the carrots — no knowing![16]

These were Catherine Macphee's memories of Michaelmas in her youth (see also p. 60).

Michael was invoked at all times of the year for help and protection, along with Brigid and Columba and Mary. He was endowed with a wide range of functions, from meeting the souls of the dead as they left the body and escorting them to heaven, to acting as patron saint of horses, and helping childless women to motherhood.

On his feast day on September 29 horse races were a central feature of the celebrations, and there was unusual license to steal other people's horses for use in the races and the circuiting of the St Michael enclosure. Women who wanted a child went sunwise round the enclosure appealing for his aid and singing his hymn, and a child born in answer to their prayers was often called a child of Michael or a carrot of Michael (referring to the fertility fun and games recalled by Catherine Macphee).

The Michael hymn

You Michael the victory-bringer,
I make my circuit under your shield,
You Michael of the white horse,
And of the bright shining swords,
That defeated the dragon,
Be you at my back,
Ranger of the heavens,
Hero of the King of all,
O Michael the victory-bringer,
My pride and my guide,
O Michael the victory-bringer,
Apple of my eye.

I make my circuit
In the companionship of my saint,
On the machair, on the meadow,
On the chill heathery hill.
Though I be crossing the ocean
And the hard globe of the world,
No harm can befall me
Beneath the circle of your shield.
O Michael the victory-bringer,
Gem of my heart,
O Michael the victory-bringer,
God's shepherd you art.

Be the holy Three of Glory
Ever at peace with me,
With my horses, with my cattle,
With the crops coming up in the fields

> Or ripening in the sheath,
> On the machair, on the moor,
> In stook, in stack, in store.
> All things high or low,
> All things inside and outside,
> Be to the holy Three of Glory,
> And to Michael victory-bringer.[17]

In another of the hymns the preoccupation with sustaining fertility through the dark dead winter to come is clear:

> You chief of chiefs, You chief of angels,
> Spread your wing over sea and land,
> For yours is their fullness, yours is their fullness,
> Your own is their fullness.[18]

There was an almsgiving circuit around the poorer neighbours as well on St Michael's Day, to give them a good start to the winter. Those who remembered the poor on that day and shared their own feast with them were called:

> the compassionate men and the generous women, who
> are taking mercy and compassion on the poor, and on the
> tearful, on the dejected and despised, on the miserable
> who need alms, and on the orphans without pith, without
> power, without support, without breast-staff, without
> leaning-rod, formed in the image of the Father all cre-
> ative. And the surprisingly white angels of God, with
> their feet on tiptoe, their eye on the horizon, their ear to
> the ground, their wings flapping, their bodies quivering,
> are waiting to send news of the deed with a beat of their
> wings to the King of the everlasting throne.[19]

Women's part in the Michaelmas celebrations shows remnants of an earlier pagan tradition under the overlay of Christian conventions about the roles of women. Occasionally the girls as well as the men were active in the horse races, and it was the women who challenged their chosen men with gifts of carrots and wishes for their virility:

"Progeny and prosperity on your lying and rising,"
said the woman, to which the man would reply as he took
the carrot gift:
"Progeny and peace on the hand that gave,
Progeny and peace on my love who gave,
Progeny and plenty without stint on your dwelling,
Mating and mothering on my brown maid,
Fortune and fruitfulness to my love who gave."

And after that, while the horse racing went on:

Here and there young men and women ride about and
wander away, converting the sandy knolls and grassy
dells of the fragrant machair into arcadian meadows and
Eden groves.

Christmas and Hogmanay

Christmas Eve was the night of the cakes, or the night of the
gifts, because that was the time for exchanging gifts in memory
of the greatest gift of the whole world, which was the gift of
Christ to humankind from God Himself. The woman of the house
made a special Christmas cake or bannock, symbolic of Christ
(*bannag* is a complex word in Gaelic which can mean a bannock
or cake, but also an offering or blessing, and in certain contexts
the Eucharist). It was mixed and baked with great seriousness
and ceremony, using completely fresh meal and none that has
been left over from previous bakings, for that would bring ill
luck. It is blessed by the woman holding it in her left palm and
turning the thumb of the right hand sunwise through the centre.
Because the bannock is a symbol of Christ it is broken and eaten
with great care and reverence, and the presiding woman places
the baking stone in her girl children's laps, in memory of the
first Christmas nursing of the baby Jesus by Brigid, and of Mary
mothering the child of heaven. A blessing on the girl children
was sung to accompany this sacramental act, but the words of
the hymn have been lost. There are still, however, carols that
bring the birth of Christ movingly down to the familiar ways of
the Western Isles, like the following, where Mary goes down on
her knee to give birth like the Hebridean women:

Hail the Bread

Hail the Bread, hail the Bread,
Hail the Bread of Life!

Fair Mary went down onto her knee,
And see now the King of glory on her breast.

The flap of the sack, the flap of the shirt
The flap of the hide upon the door,

To tell to us that Christ is born,
The Chief of Chiefs of the land of promise.

I see the hills, I see the strand,
I see the host upon the wing.

I see angels on the clouds,
Coming with speech and friendship towards us.[20]

Where the Christmas songs still lingered in Alexander Carmichael's time, they were sung by bands of young men dressed in long white shirts and tall white hats, who went around the houses to do homage to the Christ Child on Christmas Eve. They would pick up the youngest child in the house to be the baby Jesus, or failing that, make some kind of figure to carry in procession sunwise round the house on the recurring "lambskin without spot or blemish."

The "Christmas Lads" were given gifts in exchange, of bannocks and butter and crowdie. Their songs usually took the form of a Christ blessing on house and household to celebrate His coming:

Christmas chant

Listen! Listen! The blessed One!
Listen! Listen! The blessed One!
Listen, you all! Blessed the King!
Listen! Be there joy on you!

Prosperity be on this dwelling,
On all you have seen and heard,
On the bare bright floor flags,
On the fine stone stanchions standing.
Listen! Listen! The Blessed One!

Bless this house and all that it contains,
From rafter and stone and beam;
Deliver it to God from cloth to covers,
Be there health on those therein.
Listen! Listen! The Blessed One!

Be you occupying this house your live-long life,
Be you lively round the hearth;
Many be the ties and stakes about the house,
The people living on a sure foundation.
Listen! Listen! The Blessed One!

Offer up to the Being from floor to roof,
From stone to beam and beam to stone,
Offer up both battens and boards,
Be health to the people that are here.
Listen! Listen! The Blessed One!
Listen! Listen! Blessed is He!
Joy be on you![21]

There are signs of two rather contradictory traditions combining in the Christmas carousers. They seem to be linked with the old belief in Ireland and Scotland that whatever stranger came to your door on Christmas Eve should be taken into the house and given the best of fare, for it could be Christ at the door, and no good Christian would turn Him away and refuse Him a place to lay His head, as happened in that inhospitable inn in Bethlehem. But this seems to have merged with a midwinter carousing ritual, where young men dress up and go round half mocking, half well-wishing the neighbours, and demanding free bannocks and cakes and ale. That was a Hogmanay or New Year's Eve tradition which seems to have got mixed up with Christmas, though it also went on at Hogmanay, with a few variations.

Hogmanay

> We are come to the door,
> To see if we are the better for our visit,
> To tell the generous women of the place
> That tomorrow is New Year's Day.[22]

The Hogmanay Lads surround the house and climb up on the
roof with as much noise as they can muster. The walls of the old
houses were up to five feet thick, and the thatched roofs were
raised from the inner edges of these wide walls, so there was a
ledge along which the carousers cavorted to attract the attention
of the household and gain admittance. One of the crew dressed
up in the hide of a bull with horns and hoofs still on it, and his
mates struck the hide with their sticks to set up a deadly din.
Having been admitted they would take stock of the quality of
the hospitality offered them and if satisfied would process
sunwise round the fire, singing:

> May God bless the dwelling,
> Each stone and beam and stave,
> All food and drink and coverings,
> May health to you be always here.

Should they be meanly treated by the woman of the house, they
would march "widdershins" (anti-clockwise) round the fire and
stamp out, singing a curse on the household:

> The curse of God and of Hogmanay be on you,
> And the plague of the screaming buzzard,
> Of hen-harrier and raven and eagle,
> And the plague of the sneaking fox.
>
> The plague of the hound and the cat be on you,
> Of the boar, of the badger, of the bear,
> Of the hipped bear and of the wild wolf,
> And the plague of the foul foumart.

The beating of the bull hide may have been, as Carmichael

suggests, the laying of an evil spirit. It may have been the laying of the old year to bring in the new, accompanied by the necessary mockery and dressing up that secures its practitioners from evil spirits in the gap between old and new. There is also the possibility that dressing up in makeshift female attire (white shirt or smock to represent female clothes was a common device in many European countries) and cursing ungenerous hospitality was a satirical reversal of the usual roles, where women are the guardians of morality and shame their families into doing the right thing. Such cross-dressing charivaris were widespread across Europe as a way of warning folk to stick to community values.

On the first morning of the new year they celebrated with a blessing.

New Year blessing

God, bless to me the new day,
Never before granted to me;
It is to bless Your own being here,
You have given me this time, God.

Bless You to me my eye
Let my eye bless all it sees;
I will bless my neighbour,
Be my neighbour blessing me.

God, give me a clear heart,
Keep me in the sight of Your eye;
Bless to me my children and my spouse,
And bless to me my wherewithal.

Augury and divination

There were certain times of the year when it was proper to take stock of one's life and take the omens for the future, and naturally enough the quarter days were favoured, since material fortunes were then tested by rents falling due and the farm

produce stretching or not stretching to meet them. It was fitting
to assess whether the tides of fortune in every sphere of life
were flowing in favour or dragging against. Divination was also
used on special occasions of trial or difficulty or loss, however,
when a member of the household was in peril at sea, or a
precious object lost.

There was a biblical as well as a pagan basis for this belief in
omens and augury. The druids had sacrificed animals — and in
particularly heavy crises for the tribe they used human
sacrifices, watching how the scapegoat fell to read the omens for
a coming battle or the outcome of a drought. In *Ecclesiastes* did
it not say that the wise like the foolish must die, and all can
seem meaningless, a chasing after the wind? So the best a
person can do is to live with the flow of things, which are all of
God, and be mindful that:

> There is a time for everything,
> and a season for every activity under heaven:
> a time to be born and a time to die,
> a time to plant and a time to uproot,
> a time to kill and a time to heal,
> a time to tear down and a time to build,
> a time to weep and a time to laugh,
> a time to mourn and a time to dance,
> a time to scatter stones and a time to gather them,
> a time to embrace and a time to refrain
>   from embracing,
> a time to seek out and a time to give up,
> a time to keep and a time to throw away,
> a time to tear and a time to mend,
> a time to be silent and a time to speak,
> a time to love and a time to hate,
> a time for war and a time for peace.

Augury or the seeing of the unseen was primarily a means of
working out the right times for action and schemes (and for
inaction equally) in the affairs of all God's creatures. These were
discernible to the people who were blessed with the gift of the
second sight, though all might have glimmerings of this gift at

high-wrought moments. Women were thought to be blessed with
the second sight and the gift of augury more often than men in
the Gaelic culture. So when, as was their habit, the people
projected back onto the Bible stories their own way of life, they
attributed to Mary and Brigid the gift of augury. When the child
Jesus was lost it was by augury that they discovered him to be
disputing with the rabbis in the temple. This was the *frith
Mhoire*, the augury of Mary, which was turned into a prayer for
the gift of insight on life's quest for truth:

Augury of Mary

God over me, God under me,
God before me, God behind me,
I on Your road, O God,
And You in my steps, O God.

The augury Mary made of her Son,
The seeing Brigid made through her palm
Did You see it, King of life?
I saw, said the King of life.

The augury Mary made for her own child,
When He was missing a while,
Knowledge of truth, not knowledge of falsehood
Be on me to see my quest.

Son of shining Mary, King of life,
Give You me eyes to see my whole quest,
And saving grace before me,
That will not dull nor dim.[23]

The second sight was seen as a gift inherited, to be treated with
respect and reserve, only to be used on serious occasions of need
and not for frivolous purposes. It was done with much meditation and careful preparation, accompanied by Christian prayers,
even if it had come down through certain gifted families from
pagan times. For it was said to run in the family, and there was,
and is, a family name — Freer or Frere — which was associated

with *frithir,* "the children of the seer." Carmichael says of the gift that:

> It survived in the Western Isles until within modern times, but it is not now practised, though there are those who are said to have inherited the gift but do not use it for fear of the ridicule of their neighbours and the anathema of the ministers. The clergy were much averse to the practice, and stamped it out along with the rest of the picturesque lore of the people.[24]

The formal rules urged that divination should be done on the first Monday of the quarter, bare-footed and bareheaded, before sunrise, while fasting, in the name of the Mary Mother. The seer would first walk sunwise three times round the central hearth of the house in the name of Father, Son and Holy Spirit, then moving to the door she would place a hand on each door jamb and gaze out in front to take note of whatever good and bad omens could be seen. A man or woman might be seen coming towards her (a good sign) or going away (a bad sign). A beast might be rising (a good sign) or lying down (a bad sign). Account was taken of birds flying or swimming in the sea or lochs. Ravens were a sign of death, while ducks (mallards are the birds of Mary) and doves were a favourable omen. After the Reformation there was some rationalization of bird omens. Lapwings were a bad sign for Protestants since they were the birds who had betrayed the Covenanters by revealing their presence to their persecutors when they were holding their open air services on remote moorland places.

Good omens for beginning a journey were ducks, if it was a sea trip, and sheep rising. But to see goats is a sign for delaying a journey. A group of three sparrows or meadow pipits giving song near to the house means the death of a child — they are singing the requiem, and will go away after the child has died. Red hair on a passing neighbour was mischievous, for red was the colour of Judas the betrayer. A cockerel coming towards the seer means good news ...

Seeing across water, whether sea or stream or loch, was a difficult business, for it was believed that:

the *sàiol sàidh,* the race of fays, has more power under
water than above water, under the foundations of the sea
than under the foundations of the land; and the *sàiol
sàidh* interferes with the current of man's thoughts and
thwarts man's mind and wishes. The sea is more sacred
and mysterious than the land, and contains inhibiting
spirits not known ashore; therefore ... the *frith* is hard to
read.

When seeking a lost person or possession, the seer made a tube
of her hands, as Mary and Brigid had done to find the lost
Christ, and by looking through the tube of her palms she would
"see" where the missing object was. When Boswell and Johnson's
great friend Donald Maclean of Coll was drowned on a boat trip
with friends to the Innis Choinnich, the *frith* was used to
discover his body in the Sound of Ulva. And when a wife, whose
man had been away in Australia to make his fortune, wanted to
find out his fate after three years, she went to a woman seer
who told her, "Thy husband is in such a place and not where
thou didst fancy. He is safe and sound but has not prospered
and has not written to thee, but he will write to thee now and
without delay." Sure enough she got a letter three months later,
in which he asked her: "Didst thou go to Mary daughter of Neil
on such a day and at such an hour? I was stricken as I was
never stricken before and was like to die for full twenty minutes.
No one expected I should live. I saw Mary daughter of Neil
before me in the flesh as completely as ever I saw thee, and she
spoke to me ... I have not prospered in this country more than
has many another man of my kind."

In the summer of 1990 I stayed at a farmhouse on the Isle of
Skye where the woman of the house was pregnant with her
second child. She told me that the first person to tell her she
was pregnant, before she even knew herself, was a local woman
with the second sight. And, she added thoughtfully, "you
wouldn't believe it, but she's a retired university lecturer from
Edinburgh. Still, she was a Skye woman originally ..."

5. Woman of nature

Animal and bird stories

"The birds and beasts of the *Carmina Gadelica* are all of our race, and can talk and laugh, jest and moralize, with the best of us," says Carmichael. Janet Campbell of Lochskiport, South Uist, often had a cluster of children around her listening to her every word, because "birds and beasts, reptiles and insects, whales and fishes, talked and acted through her in the most amusing manner and in the most idiomatic Gaelic."[1] Through animal stories, beliefs and values were passed on to the coming generation, as in the story of the kestrel and the red fox, which was used as a warning against losing sight of the main object for the sake of a minor gain.

> The Fox got hold of the Kestrel and the Kestrel said:
> "Let me go! Let me go and I'll lay you an egg as big as your paw!" But he did not let him go an inch, not even when the Kestrel offered an egg as big as a fist, and then an egg as big as the Fox's head.[2]

Children's rhymes were often just a melodic chanting that energized their games, but they were sometimes a way of passing on the folk theology, as in the song that was sung on seeing the small yellow and white butterfly found in the Western Isles:

> Butterfly! Butterfly!
> Whose soul were you carrying,
> Butterfly, Butterfly!
> Yesterday to heaven?[3]

The Gaels observed that the yellow butterfly bore markings that could be seen as the folds of Jesus' shroud, so they held it as a sacred creature that brought good luck and was never seen in the company of the wicked. Some said it had first come into the world out of Christ's tomb at the resurrection, and it came to be an image of the angels that flew down to earth to take the souls of the dead up to heaven. So it was a good sign if it was seen in the vicinity of a house where someone had recently died. It was the *dealan-de,* the flame of God, that would bear up the dear departed one.

Instinct versus civilization

There is a blend of pagan and Christian attitudes towards the natural world, which recognizes that wild creatures have kindly instincts that "civilized" humans may have lost, and that God's own creatures can be well-disposed helpers of needy humans. The dividing line between animal and human is never firmly fixed in the Celtic tradition. Humans can behave like the most predatory animals, and animals can display the best of human qualities, safeguarding and nurturing their young, or keeping a comfortable home in adverse circumstances, like the badger in winter:

> When the badger emerges [from his set] in spring, he is
> thin and emaciated. He never comes out in the winter,
> unless upon a rare occasion when a dry sunny day may
> tempt him out to air his hay bedding. The intelligence
> with which the badger brings out his bedding, shakes it
> in the sun, airs it in the wind, and carries it back again
> to his home, is interesting and instructive.[4]

The mallard (called Mary's duck or the duck of the green head) were admired for their tender mothering of their young, and boy children were taught never to harm them during their long breeding season.

There are many tales of humans being suckled by deer when they have been cast out by humans. The deer are held to be friendly animals whose instincts are to help those especially whom misfortune has driven mad, like the Melody Woman of the Hills whose story was told in Chapter 2 (see p.68):

> On milk of deer I was reared,
> On milk of deer was nurtured,
> On milk of deer 'neath heaven's sphere,
> On crest of hill and mountain.

The Gaels believed that most of the suffering in the world is a result of human meanness and nastiness, and they made up stories to explain how nasty animals can be part of the good creation. The rat, for instance, was the consequence of a greedy woman in Palestine pretending she had nothing in order to get something out of Christ as he went through the land aiding ordinary people. She had in fact a litter of pigs and as punishment of her greed the pigs turned into rats that "rushed forth gnawing and devouring and destroying, and would have destroyed the whole world had not our Blessed Lord created the cat to check them."

But just as suffering is often the result of human cruelty and greed, so it can be diminished by humans showing compassion to wounded creatures:

> A woman found a wounded swan on a frozen lake near her house and took it home, where she set the broken wing, dressed the bleeding feet, and fed the starving bird with lintseed and water. The woman had an ailing child, and as the wounds of the swan healed the health of the child improved, and the woman believed that her treatment of the swan caused the recovery of her child.[5]

In personal celebration she composed a lullaby which blended the two strands of her joy — the recovery of the swan and the healing of her child. The refrain imitated the fluting sound of the swans flying over the lochans of the Western Isles. The speech of birds as it sounded in the Gaelic can hardly be reproduced in translation, but the elements of soft liquid sounds and repeating mournful notes are hinted at in this bit of song about another swan healing, this time attributed to St Columba, the great Celtic healer. The white swan is addressed as:

> *Bhaintighearna na tuinne,* (Lady of the wave)
>   Guile guile,
> *Bhaintighearna na tuire,* (Lady of the sorrowing)
>   Guile guile,
> *Bhaintighearna na fuinne,* (Lady of the melody)
>   Guile guile.

Attending to the world of nature

Awareness of the natural world meant paying close and continuing attention to the creatures till you knew them so well you could imitate them with affectionate exactness. Skilled pipers were able to intone the voices of the duck, the lark, the thrush and the swan, and, says Carmichael:

> I have seen men and women, boys and girls, who could sing and croon and whistle imitations of birds so affectionately that the birds themselves stood still and listened, turning their heads this way and that to ascertain whence the sound came, and tentatively, enquiringly, cautiously drawing nearer to it.[6]

A favourite character in Gaelic story-telling was *Bile-binn,* Melody-mouth, whose singing was so exquisite that "the birds of the air, the beasts of the field and the fishes of the sea stood still and listened." It was accepted that creatures, like humans, are sensitive and capable of being enchanted by the magic of music, as well as enchanting humans in turn, or at any rate offering friendly and helpful messages.

Gaelic lore is full of signs and auguries based on paying attention to the habits of the creatures, domestic or wild. The dawn cock-crow was a friendly greeting to start the day, "dispelling danger and darkness and all supernatural evil from the land." After that it was safe to travel, even if it was still dark, for all

would be well for even the timid and fearful. But a cock crowing
untimely was a bad sign, usually meaning illness or death in the
house. When the teal flew in on the seashores in winter, it
meant a bad storm and was a warning to people to secure their
homesteads against the raging gales. And those who were up
high in the mountains and saw the ptarmigan moving off from
their favourite summits above the two thousand foot mark, knew
to follow their example and descend, even in clear weather, for
there would be heavy snowfalls coming within a few hours.

Familiarity with the world of nature enriched the Gaels' way
of seeing their world, and also added to their richness of self-
expression. To have "raven knowledge" meant the knack of arriv-
ing opportunely — accidentally in time for a feast or a celebration of some kind, or at a moment when your particular skills or
gifts were needed to help out or avert disaster. Good wishing
and bad wishing often drew on the shared lore of nature. On a
dear one you could wish the "Power of eagle" or "Voice of swan
be yours, Voice of honey be yours." On a hated one you could
wish "the bursting of the serpent (or the salmon) on you," since
both split open giving birth to their young, according to a curious
belief. However, serpent and salmon may have acquired their ill-
omened reputation after the coming of Christianity, for both
were sacred creatures of the pagan druidical religion and pre-
Christian symbols of wisdom and insight, as was often acknowl-
edged in Gaelic stories of holy wells of healing and augury,
inhabited by a salmon who combined the cunning wit of a druid
with the saintly insights of a monk.

The creatures in Bible stories

In the Christian era, ancient beliefs in the goodness or badness
of creatures were justified by embroidering on the Bible stories,
so that they took on a Gaelic colouring and were given a Gaelic
context. It was alright to trample on the black beetle or grave-
digger beetle because that was the one who had betrayed
Christ's presence to Herod's soldiers when the Holy Family were
on the flight into Egypt. But the brown beetle put them off the
scent by telling a lie, so that one should never be squashed

underfoot — only turned on his back as a modest punishment for the lie he had told to save Jesus.

> When the Being of glory was in retreat,
> And wicked men in pursuit of Him,
> What said the groveller of blindness
> To the beetle and the butterfly?
>
> "Saw you passing today or last night
> The Son of my Love, the Son of God?"
> "We saw, we saw," said the black beetle,
> "The Son of freedom pass yesterday."
>
> "Wrong, wrong, wrong you are,"
> Said the holy brown beetle,
> "A long year it was last night
> Since the Son of God went by."[7]

In the Gaelic version of the early days of Christianity the founders are concerned to help animals as well as humans, as in this story of Peter and Paul blessing the birth of a faun:

The hind

> Peter and Paul were passing by,
> While a hind in the path was bearing a faun,
> "A hind is bearing there," said Peter,
> "I see it is so," said Paul.
>
> "As her foliage falls from the tree,
> So may her placenta fall to the ground,
> In name of the Father of Love and of the Son of
>   Grace,
> And of the Spirit of loving wisdom;
> Father of Love and Son of Grace,
> And Spirit of loving wisdom.[8]

The pagan Celtic world had peopled the Otherworld with animals as well as men and women, for in the Blessed Isles beyond the setting sun people who had departed this world continued to do the things they loved on earth, though with no pain and with great ease and beauty. A few descriptions of this pagan paradise lingered on into the Christian era, as this picture of Otherworld spirits on a hunting trip shows:

> ... a multitudinous host of spirits with hounds on leash and hawks on hand. The air was filled with music like the tinkling of innumerable silver bells, mingled with the voices of the Host, calling to their hounds ... [The dogs' leashes were] silver bespangled with gold and brilliant stones that sparkled in the bright moonbeams and the light of the fire.

Animals had a spirit life too, and so could not be treated cavalierly, even when they were hunted for food and also for pleasure, as happened in Gaelic lands. How then did they reconcile their love of creatures with the killing of them?

Ethics of killing animals

The practice of animal (and indeed human) sacrifice was common in the pagan Celtic world, in the belief that the shed blood, the life energies released, could be channelled into a worthy cause necessary for the well-being of the people — a good harvest, increase of flocks, or the defeat of marauding enemies. To ensure future prosperity within a building and to safeguard from evil, animals or birds (often a cat or cockerel) were buried in the foundations, and this custom continued right up till the beginning of the twentieth century in some remote parts.

The Celtic understanding of sacrifice may indeed have helped the early missionaries in the task of converting them to Christianity, for the central message of Christ's ultimate sacrifice on the cross for the sake of suffering humanity would resonate with their own world view that you cannot expect to get without giving or to achieve your particular paradise without yielding up to the universal powers their dark dues. The strange story of Columba's disciple Oran being buried alive on Iona and a chapel being built over his grave after Columba sacrificed him for the greater good of the Church, seems to stem from an intermingling of pagan and Christian beliefs about necessary sacrifice.

It follows that the Gaelic knowledge of and affection for the creatures of sea, land and sky, was much more than sentimental, for it allowed for killing them when that was justified according to their material needs and spiritual beliefs. Primarily they caught the fish and hunted the deer and the seabirds for food. Their relationship with the creatures they hunted was however a complicated blend of respect and necessary killing. Deer hunters and fishers developed a deep knowledge of the ways of the creatures they hunted, and there was a whole range of taboos which the mothers would pass on to their children through storytelling and songs. Many of these taboos show sound ecological sense long before the word ecology was commonly heard or understood.

Young boys were initiated into these hunting taboos during a ceremony when the head was anointed with oil while they stood barefoot on bare ground (in touch with the earth) and were instructed into respect for the prey they would hunt.

> He was not to take life wantonly. He was not to kill a
> bird sitting, nor a beast lying down, and he was not to
> kill the mother of a brood. Nor was he to kill an un-
> fledged bird nor a suckling beast, unless it might be the
> young of a bird or beast of prey. It was at all times
> permissible to destroy certain clearly defined birds and
> beasts of prey and evil reptiles, with their young.[9]

The parent then solemnly chanted the hunting blessing over the young boy:

> From my loins begotten were you, my son,
> May I guide you to the way that is right,
> In the holy name of the apostles eleven
> In the name of the Son of God torn by you.
>
> In the name of James, and Peter, and Paul,
> John the Baptist, and John the apostle above,

Luke the physician, and Stephen the martyr,
Muriel the fair and Mary mother of the Lamb.

In the name of Patrick holy of the deeds,
And Carmac of the rights and tombs,
Columba beloved, and Adamnan of laws,
Fite calm, and Brigid of the milk and cows.

In the name of Michael chief of hosts,
In the name of Ariel youth of lovely hues,
In the name of Uriel of the golden locks,
And Gabriel seer of the Virgin of grace.

The time you will have closed your eye,
You shall not bend your knee nor move,
You shall not harm the duck that is swimming,
Never shall you harry her of her young.

The white swan of the sweet singing,
The speckled dun of the brown tussock,
You shall not cut a feather from their backs,
Till the doom-day, on the crest of the wave.

On the wing be they always,
Before you put missile to your ear,
And the white Mary will give you of her love,
And the lovely Brigid will give you of her cattle.

You shall not eat fallen fish nor fallen flesh,
Nor one bird not brought down by your hand,
Be you thankful for the one,
Though nine should be swimming ...[10]

The hunting blessings were not only a way of instructing young boys but an affirmation that the animal world was under the protection of the saints of heaven, and as significant a part of God's creation, as the human world. It was even possible to put oneself in the position of the hunted animal rather than the hunter, though that is rarer — carrying over to the

animal world the feelings of human beings, as in this example
of bitter wit:

The hare

Whoever reads *my* testament,
I was virtuous without question,
Without gloom or servility
In my nature.

I would not nibble rank grass —
What was food for my kind
Was the tender shoots
Of the moorlands.

My cap, though it be reddish,
Was a favourite with gentle ladies,
And my haunch, though cold,
Relished by gents.

Tis a sad tale to tell
That tonight I'm laid low,
And this brain-box of mine
Is smashed up.

After they had stripped off my coat
Right down to my paws,
And roasted my carcase to a turn
On the embers.

It wasn't like this I was
At the time of Martinmas,
Frisking and sporting
Over the rough hills.

No thought at that time
That the villain would come
With his snare to entrap me
In the gloaming.

I was at home on the heaths
Where my dad and my forebears
Were cavorting, lively
And spirited,

Nibbling away at the blades of grass
On rounded slopes and moorland —
Till I fell into the snare
That was my undoing.[11]

Seal lore

Besides the close observation of creatures who are sharing the
same creation with human beings under the protection of the
same heaven, the Gaelic love of animals was expressed in a
symbolism which integrated the natural world with the human
world in story-telling. For example, the Uist people hunted seals
and used them for food and lamp oil, but they were ambivalent
about this, for there was an old belief that seals were people
under spells. They represented the possibility of shape-shifting
from human to animal or animal to human which is so common
in Celtic mythology and gives pause to the killing of creatures
who might be souls under enchantment.

Seal lore is a typical Gaelic mix of natural and supernatural
attitudes to animals. The people observed that when the seals
out on the rocks of the bays roared loudly and persistently it
was a warning of coming storms, and they used this friendly
animal message to prepare themselves. They were fully versed
in the different kinds of seals and their life cycles, calling the
small seals the tribe of elves and the great seals the tribe of
giants. They knew that the small seal bears its cub around
midsummer, a grey colour at birth with short hard bristly fur
like its mother; and that the great seal bears its cub around
midwinter, white and smooth haired for the first two months,
then moulting and growing bluish grey bristles. The small seals,
they observed, kept to the narrow straits and the indented sea-
lochs, while the great seals had their own territory out on the
open ocean among the outer isles and the skerries.

With this very practical down-to-earth knowledge of the seals
there co-existed many stories of more than ordinary affection
between people and animals, where a human falls in love with
a seal woman and she bears children but eventually is drawn
back into the Seal Kingdom because of ill treatment from her
human lover or yearning for the Otherworld. In the following
tale, the Christian message is overlaid on the pagan story, with
suitably ambivalent results for ending with an attempt to cover
the ambiguities and complexities of Gaelic attitudes to animals.

The daughter of the king of the land of the waves

There was formerly a man in Aird an Runnair in North
Uist who was called Red Roderick of the Seals. He was
out one night fishing from the rock, and he heard such
sweet delightful music as his ear had never heard. The
man followed the music and softly and dumbly listened to
it, and he was sure that never in the mortal world had he
heard the like. He saw the musicians clearly, a fine
stately company dancing while one of them played music.
They were fairly decked in the silk of Galway and the
satin of France.

Over in a rocky cleft he saw a heap of things black and
black-grey, speckled and speckled-grey, as they might be
the hides of cattle. What was here but the skins of the
seals which they had doffed at the dance. The man stood
gazing at this play, not knowing under the gentle Mary
Mother what it was or where he would go.

The music ceased. Roderick went across in haste and
put a skin under his great cloak and stood to see what
would happen next. Each and every seal took a covering
and put it on, and they rushed down to the sea one after
another as children might be seen dispersing from the
school-house, without heed one to another. One maiden
stood — the loveliest brown-haired maid on whom eye of
man ever gazed in the whole world. The maiden's person
was comely, straight and shapely as a moorland rush, her
skin as white as the snow of one night on the crests of
the peaks, her brown entwining hair of the glorious

aspect of the sun, and her two eyes warm like two honied
dew drops on the tips of the bushes. The man was thinking to himself that never in the mortal body nor in the
thought of night had he seen a blood-drop so fair as the
brown-haired maid.

She was wringing her hands and shedding tears,
ranging up and down, hither and thither, searching for
her garment, for the garment was lost. She saw not a
glimpse of it, for it was under the man's great coat.

The woman's beauty fired his heart and softened his
breast, and he went over, his bonnet in his hand, and
enquired of her what she lacked. She flamed like the
sunbeam arising in the summer's dawn, every drop of
blood in her body in her bright face. "I have lost my
beautiful garment and have not a shadow of knowledge
where it may be." "Come with myself, dear maiden, and I
will give you a garment in its place."

The brown-haired maid of beauty went home step for
step with Red Roderick. He went to the shop and bought
a suit for her and the maiden put it on. "I am," she said,
"the daughter of the King of the Land of the Waves under
spells. My mother died and my father brought home
another in her place. My stepmother said that I was in
her way and asked the floor-messenger to carry me to the
strand and leave me there. The woman did as she was
bid and struck my forehead with the magic wand and I
fell into a swoon. The first I knew on waking was that a
great band of seals was around me arraying me in every
finery that is best in the land of the waves. I should have
been there for ever were it not that you did greet me in
the name of the King of the creatures."

A cleric was found and the maiden was baptized and
married without more delay. She bore three handsome
shapely sons to the man, but the seals' blood was in
them. After a number of years she said, "I am going,
Roderick. Give me my garment, for I failed to say farewell to the folk of my love and affection at the dancing.
They will not carry me away since the blessed water is on
my face and forehead. Give you support to my three sons

and rear them with love and tenderness. Thanks to you for your kindness but take care that you kill no seal all your days lest you kill my mother or my brother or my sister on the skerry. Leave my covering on the beach and hide yourself where they will not see you. On this side of the stream, farewell."

The night of the dancing came and the seals danced heartily as of wont in the half-light of the moon. They did not touch her, for the blessed water was on her forehead.[12]

The Gaelic way of connecting animal and human lives, this world and the Otherworld, holy and unholy, is well epitomized in the old sculptures to be seen to this day on the tower of St Clement's Church, Rodel, in Harris. Round the outside of the squat square tower are carvings of fishes and reptiles, birds and animals, and a man and woman displaying their sexual natures with archaic nonchalance. No Christian Adam and Eve, these two, but a pagan pair whose display of sexual energies must in ancient times have been a promise of fertility — for people, flocks and crops alike, since all were seen as sharing the flow of life.

6. Woman of healing

Herbal healing

Throughout the history of medicine, ordinary people have gone on using herbal remedies and faith healing alongside or instead of professional medicine. Poverty is a factor, but is not enough to explain the persisting tradition of simples and specifics passed on from mother to daughter as a perennial treasure of practical everyday wisdom. Even now the World Health Organization estimates that around 85% of the world population relies heavily on herbal medicine to cure their ills, and in the West where conventional medicine is most readily available, there has been a growing enthusiasm for alternative more natural remedies since the 1970s. Why is this? Part of the answer lies in worries about high technology medical practices (in birthing and dying for instance), and about the side effects of the drug companies' products, or their addictive nature, as in the case of some widely prescribed tranquillizers. But there is, too, a growing awareness that traditional healing approaches are not all based on ignorance and magical wishful thinking, as is often claimed by the professional medical men.

Where there is an extensive use of herbal remedies still in existence today, as among the unwesternized peoples of South America, we can get some idea of the way they approach healing, to help us understand the imperfect remnants of the Gaelic healing tradition. The leading characteristics are an instinctive ability to gather healing plants from their own locality when they are sick (some domesticated animals in the West display this instinct too); a heritage of herbal remedies handed on from mother to daughter which have been tried and tested in everyday situations — part of the informal education in the household; a sense that illness is some kind of imbalance in the individual, and so mind and body and spirit must be treated as a whole; and a conviction that healing is a spiritual resource as well as a physical process.

Herbal remedies themselves have been subject to scientific scrutiny in modern times, and there have been some surprising revelations which confirm the sound instincts of many "peasant" or "backward" folk. European fur trappers and fishermen learned from the North American Indians in Newfoundland to avoid scurvy during the long winters when there were no fresh fruit or vegetables. They broke off branches of spruce in the forests and made themselves a home brew of spruce beer. So it comes as no surprise that the Gaels of the long dark Scottish winters did the same. Beer brewed from heather tops and spruce twigs is mentioned in their oral lore as one of the delights of old-time feasting and ceilidhs. Neither of these communities could have explained that vitamin C cures or prevents scurvy, but their instincts towards a healthy body and their practical ability to pick the right plants were sound enough.

Even more surprising, in view of one's initial revulsion at the use of human or animal urine in some old natural remedies, is that long before hormone replacement therapy (HRT) became a popular theme in women's magazines in the late twentieth century, explaining how menopause problems can be alleviated by modern drugs, the urine of pregnant women or animals was known by herbalists to supplement hormone deficiencies. Some of the HRT treatments currently produced by the drug companies are still making use of mares' urine, even if now women can swallow nice neat pills instead of a gagging concoction of the real thing.

Although many of the same plants occur the world over in the herbal lore of the wise woman or shaman, different stories grew up to explain why the plants have healing powers. The explanations reflect the spiritual beliefs of the specific time and place, and cope with changeovers from one religion to another, too. So when Christianity came to the Gaelic lands some of the plants which had been used by pagan druid healers or were sacred to their religion, were given a new justification. St John's Wort, for example, a plant known to be valuable for healing wounds and skin eruptions, was called the fairy herb, but also named after St John the Baptist, on the grounds that it was in bloom on his day, June 24. It retained its reputation as well for keeping evil spirits at bay, only now these were the emissaries of the devil of Christianity rather than pagan demons.

The rowan and ivy which were sacred trees to the druids continued to be favoured by the Christian Gaels for protecting livestock from mischance. Ivy, rowan and honeysuckle were often woven into a three-ply circle of protection and placed over the doors of byres and under the milk vessels to keep off both physical and spiritual evils from the domestic animals and their produce. It is here that we get into the blurred edges between magical practice and Christian protective encompassing, and it is best to let the Gaelic healers speak for themselves. Catherine Maclean of Gairloch explained it like this:

> The people used to mock me, saying that I had witch-craft. But I had no witchcraft, nor anything in creation except the power that God gave me, the God of life and of the worlds, to Whom I prayed to increase my love, to confirm my serious intent, to bless my words and to strengthen my hands. And God did that; the glory be to Him and not to me.[1]

It was impossible for a people who expressed their spirituality through the ordinary everyday activities, to draw a clear dividing line between their herbal medicine, their part-pagan runes and their faith healing. Healing was a spiritual as well as a practical activity which demanded of the healer not just plant knowledge but a quiet and serious intent, undivided attention, and faith in a power greater than themselves. They were usually unwilling to receive money for healing, since they believed that no commercial profit should be made out of human suffering. But anybody who received their healing should unobtrusively make a gift to the healer according to their means, be it only a bit of everyday home produce — a chicken or a jar of jam or a bannock cake.

The quiet ingathering of healing energies began when the healer went out to gather the healing plants. As in pre-Christian times it was thought best to gather the plants at the time of a waxing moon when the sap would be rising, in silent concentration, and in ritual purity, that is, while fasting and having washed the feet. It was better to come on the needed plant by accident than to set out deliberately to search it out. Once the gathering was done, the healer should give thanks to the good earth for yielding it, and go away without looking back, taking no more than was necessary.

The coming of Christianity confirmed the old pagan beliefs about the healing powers of plants, for was not everything the creation of the God of Life and the King of the Elements, and were not human beings put on this earth to give thanks for the creation and use it respectfully and positively? Isabel Mac-Eachainn of Bunessan on Mull put it in these words:

> Great is the virtue that is in the plants of the ground and
> in the fruits of the sea, were we but to hold them in
> esteem and turn them to good use. O King, great indeed!
> The Being of Life never set a thing in the creation of the
> universe but he set some good within it, he never did. O
> King, many a good is in the soil of the earth and in the
> depths of the sea, did we but know how to make good use
> of them ...[2]

Identification of the good creation and natural healing is expressed too in this praise poem to Jesus, which emphasises the model of Jesus as healer, who is behind all human efforts at healing:

> It were as easy for Jesus
> To renew the withered tree,
> As to wither the new
> Were it His will to do it.
> Jesus, Jesus, Jesus,
> Fit it is to praise You.
>
> There is no plant in the ground
> But is full of His virtue,
> There is no form in the strand

But is full of His blessing.
Jesus, Jesus, Jesus,
Fit it is to praise You.

There is no life in the sea,
There is no creature in the river,
There is nothing in the firmament
But is saying His goodness.
Jesus, Jesus, Jesus,
Fit it is to praise You.

There is no bird on the wing,
There is no star in the sky,
There is nothing under the sun
But is saying His goodness.
Jesus, Jesus, Jesus,
Fit it is to praise You.[3]

Safeguarding and encompassing

Thankfulness for the goodness of creation did not however lead
to any complacency about life among the Gaels. Their material
lives were harsh and none were free of want and suffering at
every stage of their living, whether or not they had at the end
the blessing of a pillow death instead of death through mishap
on water or on crag. No wonder then that there is an everpresent consciousness of irrational fate which can strike at any
moment to change the course of one's life from one day to the
next; and an everpresent need for safeguarding from the woes of
the world — the death of one's man or one's child, sickness of
livestock, failure of harvest, or powerlessness in the face of
landowner or legal system that was different from heaven's
justice. In pagan days the Gaels had sacrificed animals and
sometimes human scapegoats to ward off such disasters from
their tribe. With the coming of Christianity they developed new
invocations for safeguarding which often blend pagan and
Christian into a new synthesis, as in the many prayers of
encompassing.

The *caim* or encompassing was a way of encircling oneself or another with the spiritual protection of the Trinity or St Brigid, or Mary or Columba, so as to keep at bay danger or distress, death and doom and the malice of ill-disposed persons. In the nineteenth century, says Alexander Carmichael:

> Protestant or Catholic, educated or illiterate, make the *caim* in fear, danger or distress ... the suppliant stretches out the right hand with the forefinger extended, and turns around sunwise as if on a pivot, with the tip of the outstretched finger, while invoking the desired protection. The circle encloses the suppliant and accompanies him as he walks onward, safeguarding from all evil without or within.[4]

The words uttered could be very specific or very comprehensive, depending what was causing fear. Here is the second half of a very extended protection invoking the Graces:

> The shield of Michael is over you,
> King of the bright angels,
> To shield you and to circle you
> From your summit to your sole.
>
> Man shall not,
> Woman shall not,
> Lad shall not,
> Girl shall not
>
> Make glance nor wish,
> Hate nor envy,
> Love spell nor look,
> Spite nor trap
>
> That will smash you,
> That will suppress you,
> That will crush you,
> That will distress you.

Host shall not make,
False friend shall not make,
The fays shall not make,
The world shall not make

Missile nor launcher,
Sling nor shaft,
Axe nor arrow,
Hook nor hammer,

That will affect you,
That will afflict you,
That will harass you,
That will outmatch you.

No smith shall make,
No craftsman shall make,
No mason shall make,
No wright shall make

Gear nor gadget,
Device nor design,
Tackle nor trick,
Scheme nor strategy,

Of copper nor stone,
Of brass nor iron,
Of wood nor bronze,
Of gold nor silver,

That will check you,
That will block you,
That will break you,
That will subject you,

Here nor there,
Earth nor land,
Hither nor thither,
Up nor down,

Above nor below,
Sea nor shore,
In the sky of heaven,
In the deeps beneath.

You kernel of my heart,
You face of my sun,
You harp of my music,
You crown of my sense.

You are the love of the God of Life,
You are the love of tender Christ,
You are the love of Holy Spirit,
You are the love of each living creature,
The love of each living creature.[5]

Healing plants

Some plants used in protecting and healing were considered
blessed by association with some part of the Christian story. The
"blessed bramble" was one of these, for it was said that Christ
used a bramble stick to drive his ass on the ride into Jerusalem,
and to drive the money changers from the Temple. The
blackberries gathered off the bramble were indeed a practical
and versatile fruit, a down-to-earth blessing of the useful kind,
for they provided the wherewithal for tarts and jellies and syrup
for winter coughs. The leaves were infused for a medicinal tea,
and the roots were used for dyeing cloth. So old herbal remedies
were absorbed into Christian healing.

St John's wort was called *achlasan Chaluim-chille,* the armpit
package of Columba, the charm of Columba, the jewel of
Columba, and sometimes *alla Mhoire,* the noble plant of Mary.
Columba was said to have worn the plant on him in affection
and respect for John the Baptist who had gone about preaching
the coming of Christ. It gave protection therefore from wicked
enchantments, evil spirits and danger of death, from its double
associations with John the Baptist and Columba, the dearest

saint of the Gaels, who had been a pilgrim for Christ's sake, as John the Baptist had lived on locusts and wild honey in the wilderness for Christ's sake. Women sowed bunches of St John's wort into their bodices under the left armpit, to ensure peace and plenty in house and homestead, growth and increase in family and field. If the plant was growing in the fold of the flocks it was a sign that the livestock would flourish that year. On coming across it, the finder would recite a rune in celebration of their good fortune as they plucked it for medicinal use or as a general safeguard:

Columba's plant

Plantlet of Columba,
Without seeking, without searching,
Plantlet of Columba,
Ever under my armpit,

For luck of men,
For luck of means,
For luck of making wishes,
For luck of sheep,
For luck of goats,
For luck of birds,
For luck of fields,
For luck of shell-fish,
For luck of fish,
For luck of produce and cattle,
For luck of offspring and people,
For luck of fighting and overcoming,
On land, on sea, on ocean.

By the Three on high,
By the Three at hand,
By the Three with no end,
Plantlet of Columba,
I gather you now,
I gather you now.[6]

Flowers and leaves of St John's wort were used extensively all over Europe for treating wounds until its use declined in the eighteenth century. In Gerard's famous Herbal of 1597, the master surgeon writes that the plant if pressed or

> stamped, put into a glasse with oile olive, and set in the hot sun for certain weeks together, and then strained from those herbs, and the like quantitie of new put in and sunned in like manner, doth make an oile of the colour of blood, which is a most pretious remedie for deep wounds.

Modern herbalists have brought it back into use, and St John's Wort (Hypericum) ointment is generally available in whole food and health food shops as a balm for cuts and minor burns and for aching pains like rheumatism and sciatica. Infusions of the herb are recommended for emotional stress and strain, including premenstrual tension and menopausal depression.

Herbal healers in the Western Isles used plants that were good-omened by Christian association, and avoided those that were ill-omened by the same token. This meant that certain plants were lucky or "crossed" because they had played a good or a bad part in the telling or the retelling of the Christian story. So the reed was crossed because it had carried the sponge soaked in vinegar that was offered in jeering to Christ on the cross. The thorn tree was crossed because it had been used to make the crown of thorns for the King of Kings, and the aspen was crossed because it was the wood the cross was made of, and its quivering leaves betray its continuing guilt.

On the other side, the four-leaved shamrock was a rare and precious find because of its double associations with Mary and with the pagan goddess Epona who had presided over horses and fertility and fruitfulness. This connection between Epona and the shamrock gave rise to the belief that lucky shamrock would spring up if you planted in the ground the substance coughed up by new-born foals. Those who were lucky in finding the plant would have the "seven joys" recited in this thanksgiving rune:

You little shamrock of fair futures
Beneath the bank growing,
Where once stood the kindly Mary
The Mother of God.

The seven joys are on you,
And not a trace of evil
On you, you unsurpassed one
Of the sunbeams —

Joy of health
Joy of friends
Joy of cattle
Joy of sheep
Joy of sons
Joy of daughters,
Joy of peace,
Joy of God.[7]

The most valued plant for wide protection was the *mothan,*
which has been identified as the pearlwort or thyme-leaved
sandwort, a little tufty plant with five-petalled white flowers and
narrow leaves. It was sown into women's bodices and men's
vests under the left armpit, to give safeguarding on journeys, or
against any risky ventures, even lawsuits. Such was its power
that on occasion even the guilty might be found innocent as a
result of cajoling the protection of *mothan* on their way to court.
In the case of one Red Roderick, acquitted at the Sheriff's Court
in Lochmaddy, though "guilty of the guilt as the son of a sinner,"
the accused had bullied a charitable neighbour woman into
giving him the plant. "King of the moon, and of the sun, and of
the beautiful sublime stars, what could I myself say or do, and
the bad man in his black trouble, in his red difficulty and in his
hard plight," she said afterwards, defending her misguided compassion.[8]

The *mothan*'s protective powers seem to have come down to
the Christian Gaels from their pagan predecessors, for the plant
is especially held effective against the evil eye, the malevolence
of the Otherworld fairies and inexplicable blows of fortune. But

as usual the original reasons for its efficacy as a sacred plant of the druids probably, are overlaid with stories more fitting to Christian belief. The *mothan* was blessed, they said, because when Christ came down to earth it was the first plant he stepped on (or the first plant his foot touched when he rose from the dead). Or it had been, others said, the plant that safeguarded Mary and the Baby on the flight into Egypt. So it was happily absorbed into healing lore and gathered with the blessing of the Trinity and the saints, as in this gathering rune:

> I will pluck the pearlwort
> Under the white sun of Sunday,
> Under the kindly hand of Mary,
> And she safeguarding me,
> In the power of the Trinity
> Who gave it to grow.
> While I shall keep the pearlwort,
> Without wile shall be my lips,
> Without guile shall be my eye,
> Without harm shall be my hand,
> Without hurt shall be my heart,
> Without heaviness shall be my death.[9]

Many of the more down-to-earth remedies were used regularly for common illnesses, unlike the all-healing *mothan*, the cosmic panacea. The more common of these are again in favour, for it has been discovered that there are good reasons behind their use, as in the following examples:

Carrigean moss is a seaweed that was used for making milk puddings. It is now known that it is a source of iron and other mineral traces, and it is available in dried form in health food shops, as well as enjoying a revival in Ireland as a pudding for health-conscious tourists.

Burdock was widely used for toning people up and for cleansing the blood. An extract of the root was given for pulmonary complaints. The root, it is now known, is more powerful than the leaves, and an extract is used for clearing up skin complaints (by cleansing the blood and so toning the skin from within).

Nettles were used three times daily to cleanse the system, especially in the spring when people were debilitated after the long dark winter. Nettle infusions are now recommended for anaemia, for improving breast milk in weak mothers, and for healing poor skin caused by sluggish circulation. It is now possible to buy nettle teabags in health food shops, where in the old days you boiled up fresh nettles for broth, or made nettle beer.

Purging flax was used as the name implies for an emetic and purgative. "As much as fills the fork between the thumb and forefinger is pulled and then dried; it is pulled in the summer dog days." It has been used for this purpose throughout the history of herbal medicine, for so it is listed on one of the very first records, an ancient Egyptian papyrus of medical herbs.

Ragwort, or ragweed, was made into a poultice to heal sprains and bad cuts, by pounding up the female flowers with neat's foot oil. The male ragweed was used to keep rats out of the corn stook, by putting in layers at intervals while building the stook, so that rats would be repelled by the strong pungent smell. Alternative poultices for dressing cuts and sores which had begun to fester were made of buttercups or March chickweed (Mary's flower). The poultices were made by heating up the plants by the fire till they could be beaten into a paste that was not runny and could be kept on the sore place with a cloth binding.

Neat's foot oil is now mainly sold in Great Outdoors shops to put on leather boots as a preservative and waterproofer. In the old days when people went barefoot in the Highlands and Islands it was applied direct to the feet for relieving blisters and bruises. It was a versatile remedy however, for it was also taken internally to soothe sore throats. The woman of the house made her neat's foot oil as part of housekeeping, by boiling up cows' feet on the fire till the oil came to the surface and could be skimmed off with a saucer.

Yarrow was another remedy with a wide range of applications, including one of a rather vague though auspicious kind. If you were going on a journey, you knelt on the ground, put your hand on the plant and said "In the name of the Father, Son and Spirit" so that your journey would be blessed and "everyone will be pleasant to you, and pleasantness will be in your face." But yarrow was used specifically for sweating out fevers and for drying up wounds, and both have been found valuable by proven experience in other places too. When there was a shortage of dressings during the first World War in military hospitals they used yarrow to clear up wounds, and it is prescribed by modern herbalists for feverish conditions and for menstrual problems (by assisting the menstrual flow).

Healing charms

Although their treatments were a blend of faith and magic runes and practical herbalism, the Gaels had the beginnings of a system to explain the ills they saw around them and experienced personally in their own lives. Their belief was that there were twenty-four diseases in man and beast, caused by:

> *fridich bheaga bhideach bhronach, lan nimhe neamha*
> *agus naimhdeis,* microbes small, minute, miserable, full
> of spite, venom and hostility ... How they inherited these
> diseases the people do not know, but they think it to be
> probably through their own and their fathers' long
> continuance in offending God that these family afflictions
> come about — some families and animals being more
> afflicted than others.[10]

To offset this legacy of God's retribution for human wrong-doing, the Gaels had an optimism about their God, too — they believed that the God of Life had put into the natural creation the wherewithal to relieve these diseases, and if your faith and your perseverance were strong enough, you would come on the right remedy. But it was a search that had to be carried out in seriousness and with scrupulous attention to the respect due to God and your co-humans. For as a healer you are only an instrument of higher grace and are nothing in your own right. There are a number of healing runes which put the healers in the position of modelling themselves on Christ or Mary or Columba or Brigid, the great healers of heaven who have also healed on earth. Healing then becomes the Imitation of Christ *par excel-*

lence, or the Imitation of Brigid and the favourite Celtic saints, as in this charm for sprains:

> Brigid went out
> In the dawn of day
> With a pair of horses
> And one broke a leg.
>
> That was trouble and fuss, that
> Was tearing and loss, but
> She put bone to bone,
> She put flesh to flesh,
> She put sinew to sinew,
> She put vein to vein.
> As she healed that,
> Let me heal this.[11]

If a charm failed it was put down to frivolity of purpose or lack of faith. A woman who failed the first time to clear the eye of a herring fisher on Loch Hourn, but had a second try and was successful said: "It was wicked lack of faith that came on me and lay like a black shadow on my soul; but I prayed the God of grace to aid me and help me and to give my power back to me, and ... He did so. Look you, there is the mote that was in the eye." And she showed a little basin of water with a herring scale lying on the surface of it.[12]

Some of the healers would not give away their runes to the merely curious, however good their motives, just as the druidical healers had once kept their lore unwritten and secret, passing it on only to those who were ready to receive it and who would use it only for its intended purpose. On one occasion when Alexander Carmichael had travelled all the way from Edinburgh to Knoydart to record the healing runes of an old wise woman called Mary Cameron, she would tell him nothing for "the *eolas,* charm, was entrusted to her for no foolish purpose, and she was not going to impart it for any foolish purpose ..."

In many healing runes the feeling is that the hurt or disease is something evil that has found its way into the body and can be shifted out of it if the right formula is found and applied in the right spirit. In some of the spells said for curing consumption the idea is clearly enough expressed, as in this charm from Isabel MacEachainn of Mull:

Charm for the chest seizure

Power of moon have I over you,
Power of sun have I over you,
Power of rain have I over you,
Power of dew have I over you,
Power of sea have I over you,
Power of land have I over you,
Power of stars have I over you,
Power of planets have I over you,
Power of universe have I over you,
Power of skies have I over you,
Power of saints have I over you,
Power of heaven have I over you,
Power of heaven and power of God have I over you,
Power of heaven and power of God over you.

A part of you be on the grey stones,
A part of you on the steep mountains,
A part of you on the swift waterfalls,
A part of you on the gleaming clouds,
A part of you on the ocean whales,
A part of you on the meadow beasts,
A part of you on the marshy swamps,
A part of you on the bog-cottoned moors,
A part on the great surging sea —
She herself the best one to bear it,
The great surging sea,
Herself the best one to bear it.[13]

Consumption or tuberculosis was endemic in the Highlands and Islands, probably as a result of the damp old houses and the crowding together of big families, especially when food was scarce. The people dreaded the "chest seizure" or "hollow disease," as it was called, for they thought it was caused by the bones of the thorax closing inwards and pressing upon "heart, lungs and liver, constricting them and reducing their blood supply, and causing consumption and death." One form of treatment therefore was a powerful massage with seal oil or neat's foot oil or oil of heron or crane. As one healer put it:

> He is taking the flesh and the bones and the sinews and
> the joints asunder, and rubbing oil or butter or cream
> into the sick person, and driving it through the hardness.
> All this is great work, but to do this rightly is work of
> hands and head and heart — Mary, that is the work
> indeed.[14]

To enable this holistic approach to have its effect, the tuberculosis patient often went to live in the house of the healer, drinking the warm milk from the cow, eating tender meat cut up small, staying as much as possible in the open air while "keeping at the back of the wind and in the face of the sun."

The healers who gave the daily massage had their own preparations to make as well as their charms to utter over the patient. They would bend down and place their two palms on the ground to get in touch, and at the end they would wash their hands in running water, to draw new energy from the earth and to wash away the burden of the disease that they had drawn out of the sufferer. But at the same time many healers were close observers and understood how illness spread and its connections with living conditions:

> How the hatching mother of the *grig* or microbe got into
> the flesh and blood of a person and grew there it was not
> easy to understand nor easy to explain; but one thing —
> where there were ill care and ill keeping the hatching
> *grig* was there, running from person to person and from
> house to house like the wont of an ill tale.[15]

The treatment of thyroid deficiency among the Gaels is another example of how they blended their healing lore and their spiritual beliefs. When a child had an underactive thyroid gland, they would be stunted in mind and body. The remedy was to give them extract of the thyroid gland taken from a sheep. But not any old sheep would do. They were careful to look for a sheep, or better still a lamb, that had been born on St Brigid's day, February 1. They were satisfied when they found this "lamb of Brigid of the flocks and of the blessings," and they sacrificed the animal for the curing of the child. The thyroid extract got in this way would be specially effective, for it was blessed by Brigid in its healing work, as well as being part of God's creation which was capable of providing cures for every ill that struck, if used in the right spirit.

The treatment of skin cancers with a hemlock plaster was rather more dubious, for hemlock is a powerful poison and now on our official List of Poisons. But it was the very poison in it that they used to counteract the powerful poison of the cancer, and it has been cautiously used throughout herbal healing history to draw out "wheals, pushes and creeping ulcers that arise of hot, sharp tumours," as Culpeper describes it in his *Pharmacopaea* in the seventeenth century. In the Gaelic healing:

> A cold poultice of hemlock was applied to a cancer sore.
> The hemlock plaster was so hot and strong that it drew
> the cancer out from the bottom, the roots coming with the
> cancer as the roots come with the hemlock itself out of
> the ground.[16]

In another case of lip cancer, "the flesh containing the cancer came away, carrying the roots with it. These were very numerous and resembled the fine thready roots of hemlock." The old herbal healers' belief in the Doctrine of Signatures is evident here — the conviction that nature marks plants with signs that tell the careful observer what disease they will cure.

The healing of livestock

Farm animals were counted as part of the household and their safeguarding and healing was seen as no different from human healing in principle and in practice. In the earliest black houses they shared the same roof with the family, and their well-being was the crofting family's fortune. They were precious therefore in many senses — as the family's livelihood but also their named daily companions to whom they crooned and whom they blessed with the rest of the household. They were members, too, of the King of Life's creation. The Gaels therefore readily invoked the protection of Columba and Brigid and Mary for their animals as well as themselves. The woman or girl driving the cows out to the pasture after the morning milking had a repertoire of songs which the cattle became so familiar with that it was said they had their own favourites, as they did in the milking croons.

Driving the cows

> Closed to you be every pit,
> Smooth to you be every slope,
> Snug to you be every bare bit
> On the cold mountainside.
>
> Encircling of Mary Mother be yours,
> Encircling of Brigid the beloved be yours,
> Encircling of Michael the valiant be yours,
> Lively and full be you gathered home.
>
> Safeguarding of handsome Cormac be yours,
> Safeguarding of Brendan of the ships be yours,
> Safeguarding of Maol Duinne the saint be yours,
> In boggy ground and rocky ground.
>
> Companionship of Mary Mother be yours,
> Companionship of Brigid of cows be yours,
> Companionship of Michael the Valiant be yours,
> In your nibbling and your chewing and your
> munching.[17]

For the sheep too there were blessings to be crooned when they were moved to new pastures or gathered for the lambing or shearing. The Holy Family were for the Hebrideans people like themselves, so it was unimaginable that Mary did not have her own sheep to mind.

Blessing on the sheep

The blessing placed by Mary
On her own flock of sheep,
Against hawks, against foxes,
Against beasts, against men,
Against hounds, against thieves,
Against pole-cats, against marten-cats,
Against the evil eye, and envy,
Against disease, against dearth.
In the hollow of your gathering
Be yours the aiding of God,
On the hillock of your lying
Whole be your rising.[18]

Plants that were cure-alls for people were considered to be cure-alls for the animals as well, so in pastures where the *mothan,* pearlwort, was found, or the St John's wort, there was thanksgiving and reassurance that the livestock would have a good year, provided you safeguarded them in the byre and fold with a triple garland of sacred plants such as rowan, ivy and honeysuckle or mountain juniper. These would be placed over the lintel of the door with a prayer for protection to Columba or Brigid, for "Colum Cille was the world's head of wisdom and the head of healing of the universe" and Brigid was the compassionate, safekeeping mother and companion woman in everything to do with fruitfulness and flowering — as pre-Christian goddess and Christian saint.

St Brigid's charm

The charm put by Brigid of the graces,
On her goats, on her sheep, on her cows,
On her horses, on her chargers, on her herds,
Early and late, to and from home,

To keep them from rocks and ridges,
From the heels and horns of one another,

From the birds of the Red Rock,
And from the host of the Fiann,

From the blue peregrine hawk of Crag Duilion,
From the brindled eagle of Ben Ard,
From the hurtling hawk of Tordun,
From the sour raven of Bard's Crag,

From the fox of the tricks,
From the wolf of the heights,
From the stinking fumart,
And from the ranging wide-hipped bear ...
From every hoofed one of four feet
And from every hatched one of two wings.[19]

The figwort was another plant put under milk crocks and in the byre to increase the milk yield. The plant is called in Gaelic *lus an torranain,* the plant of the thunderer, and this Thunderer was a pagan Celtic god. But there was also a Celtic Christian saint called Torranan who became the missionary saint who converted the people of Uist, having landed there by the winds of heaven blowing his coracle on shore after he had been spurned by the Irish, as the tale went. This Torranan or Ternan has rival claims with the pagan Thunderer in the naming of the figwort, so there is once again a pagan and a Christian explanation for its healing power.

A further explanation of the figwort's power to increase the milk yield of the cows is based on the Doctrine of Signatures — something in the appearance of the plant which suggests where it will be effective. In the last generation of belief in the old plant remedies, these conflicting strands became diluted and confused, as this faint-hearted hope in the figwort by an island woman shows:

The figwort is a blessed plant. It grows in sight of the
sea. Its root is a cluster of four bulbs like the four teats of
a cow. The stalk of the plant is as long as the arm, and
the bloom is as large as the breast of a woman, and as
pure white as the driven snow of the hill. It is full of the

milk of grace and goodness and of the gift of peace and
power, and fills with the filling and ebbs with the ebbing
tide. It is therefore meet to cull the plant with the flow
and not with the ebb of the restless sea. If I had the *torranan* it would ensure me abundant milk in my cow all
the year. Poor as I am, I had rather than a Saxon pound
that I had the blessed *torranan*. I went away to John the
son of Feararchar, who knows every plant that comes
through the ground, to see if he would get me the *torranan* of power.

But John's wife said no, and that I was only a silly
woman ...[20]

But some of the old figwort gathering runes remain, as in the
following:

> I will pluck the figwort,
> With the fullness of sea and land,
> At the flow and not the ebb-tide,
> With your hand, Mary mild.
>
> The kindly Columba guiding me,
> The good Oran protecting me,
> And Brigid of generous women
> Will put fruiting in the cattle.
>
> As the King of kings laid down,
> To put milk in breast and gland,
> As the Being of life laid down,
> To put sap in udder and teat.
>
> In udder of badger,
> In udder of reindeer,
> In udder of sow,
> In udder of mare.
>
> In udder of sow,
> In udder of heifer,
> In udder of goat and ewe,
> Of roe deer and cow.

With milk, with cream, with substance,
With rutting, with begetting, with bearing,
With female calves surpassing,
With offspring, with enjoying, with blessing.

Without man of evil wish,
Without woman of evil eye,
Without malice, without envy,
Without one bad blow.

In name of the apostles twelve,
In name of the Mother of God,
In name of Christ Himself,
And of Patrick.[21]

Healing springs and holy wells

There is plenty of evidence from votive offerings of coins and jewellery and valuable weapons, and from surviving well-dressing customs, that wells and springs have been centres of power and healing for both the pagan and Christian Celts. Offerings were once made to water gods and goddesses to cure disease and to bring good luck, and anyone who dared to steal from water hoards was given a horrible death to punish the sacrilege. The spirits of the wells were particular and local, but all were connected with the profound powers of below ground, the underworld of Mother Earth, source of fundamental energies. Often the sacred wells had friendly animals or fish (the salmon or trout of wisdom) guarding them, and a holy tree to tie offerings to — as is still done at some local wells in Ireland to this day, but the offerings tend to be the bandage off a wound to remind the saint of the well of the part suffering, and coins are dropped in the water. It was very bad medicine to cut down the sacred tree or to injure or kill the presiding fish of a holy well.

Christianity took over many of the old water cults, which were held in lasting affection by local communities. The wells provided places of pilgrimage and centres of healing, and offers of thanksgiving to the now Christian presiding saint could still be made in return for healing or good fortune. Church councils in the middle ages did their best to discourage or stamp out pagan practices to do with sacred trees and offerings to holy wells. But the science of the time was unable to make clear distinctions between chemistry and alchemy, between magic and medicine in the use of healing wells. So the magical rituals continued alongside the Christian rituals and the Church was not too worried unless there was discovered to be overt worshipping of pagan gods or goddesses at the wells.

In the Highlands and Islands every district had its own healing well, *tobar slainte,* and they were widely resorted to, at least till the end of the nineteenth century. Some are still visited by pilgrims, however off the beaten track, for in 1992 I found one of Columba's holy wells in Ardnamurchan with a modern mug left carefully in a niche for drinking of the waters. Some of the wells had general healing powers, covering the whole range of human ills, from disease to lack of a lover to material disasters of crops or cattle or fishing boat. Others were for particular problems, like childlessness. At Strolamus in Skye a woman would take the water at dawn and recite a rune:

> The water of the source be on my forehead ...
> Lift you off me your mischievous fortune,
> For the wish of the woman of hurry is on me.[22]

At another holy well in Skye, at Elgol, both wife and husband went to drink the waters and ask the divinity for the gift of children, which is an unusual recognition of their shared responsibility for infertility. As has been the pervasive tendency in Gaelic approaches to healing, the woman who wanted a child would take herbal remedies as well as taking a trip to the holy well, and valerian roots were recommended in the broth, as well as water cress, or Mary's cress. Valerian is used by modern herbalists to relieve strain and stress. Gaelic wise women, I suppose, made the connection between tranquillity and nourishment, and the capacity to conceive, while at the same time taking it as a blessing.

The evil eye

Water cures were used to counteract the evil eye as well as healing physical illness and undoing bad luck. But for the evil eye cure, running water had to be fetched at dawn from a boundary stream over which the living and the dead had passed; or from below a crossing point where three streams meet. The water thus fetched was sprinkled over the affected person or animal in a Christianized rune which invoked the Trinity and the saints, but was very unchristian in sending the evil eye back on the sender, rather than turning the other cheek. Mary Ross of Bonar Bridge described the ritual in this way:

> You will sprinkle the water, pure, cold, surpassing, upon the backbone of the animal on which the evil eye has rested. And every whit of this you will do:
>
> > In the eye of God,
> > In the love of Jesus,
> > In the heed of Spirit,
>
> The Three of power. And the little drop of water left in the crock you will pour behind the fire flag. And every whit of this you will do in the eye and in the love of the Three above you. And ... I will go bound ... that your animal will be whole and healthy, and that he will rise on his four feet, and that he will begin to nibble the grass under his feet, without moan in his head nor hurt in his body, and that he will win victory over the wicked woman who put the evil eye on him.
>
> The curse was turned back on the sender in these words:
> > Your failing be on the fire flags,
> > Your sickening on the evil she.[23]

The evil eye at first sight seems to be definitely in the realm of black magic, and far away from religion. But it is worth recalling that the problem of undeserved suffering is a central one for all religions, and that the Church personified chance or deliberate mischief and evil in the shape of the Devil, that cunning but misguided angel of heaven, now fallen into the Hell of his own making. The Gaels had their own way of explaining how evil and suffering may attack even the well-doer, the Christian woman or man. You needed more than goodness and reason in life — you needed luck as well. But luck was a two-sided coin which could bring good or evil at the toss. If it brought good you could thank heaven, but if it brought evil you had to find a way of explaining it that exonerated the saints and angels. So it was put down to the evil eye of the black guile, the women and men who for one reason or another were filled with envy and wickedness and took it out on their innocent neighbours. It might not always be the black ones' fault, for there are stories about unfortunates who cannot help putting the evil eye on animals as they go about the township, and are ashamed to find out what they have done. "Most likely the poor fellow could not help it ... Go and make the man return that he may repel the evil eye," said a kindly grandmother of the house after the visit of a neighbour during which their horse fell down as if dead. "The man returned with shame and confusion, with disgrace and flushing of cheek, saying that he could not in the least help what had befallen the mare," and remedied it by going three times round the stricken beast with a rune of aiding and a prayer to the Trinity. The evil eye became a parable on the nature of evil in the world.

Whatever was responsible for the evil and suffering, aid and comfort could be had from heaven, so the runes against the evil eye appeal to God for help, while at the same time turning the eye back on the sender.

> I make to you, my dearest ... [Say name of person
>   or animal]
> The charm of Mary, the charm of the King of all kings,
> The most perfect charm that is in the world,
> Which You have given me, God of all gods,
>
> Against small eye, against big eye,
> Against eye of swift voracious women,
> Against eye of swift rapacious women,
> Against eye of swift avaricious women,

Against my own eye,
Against your own eye,
Against the eye of the grey man
Who came yesterday to the door.

Whoever it was brought you to this sorry state
With eye, with malice, with jealousy, with envy,
May her life not be prolonged
On the waves of Loch Leargain.

Be it lying on their own eyes,
Be it lying on their own sorceries,
Be it lying on their own envies,
Be it lying on their own jealousies.

Be it lying on their cow calves,
Be it lying on their bull calves,
Be it lying on their fold of young cattle,
Be it lying on their foaling mares.

Be it lying on their little children,
Be it lying on their big children,
Be it lying on their bleating goats,
Be it lying on their woolly sheep.

Be it lying on their potent men,
Be it lying on their pregnant women,
Be it lying on their virile sons,
Be it lying on their conceptive daughters.

Be it lying on the vertebrae of their spine,
Be it lying on their Achilles heel,
Be it lying on everything in the world
That these people love best of all.

But be your groaning and grief,
Your yawning and heaving,
Your sadness and your tears,
Your misery and moaning,

Be all them on the spoilers of the wings,
Be they on the beasts of the braes,
Be they on the searchers of the branches,
Be they on the wasted heath of the hills,

Be they on the ranging beasts of the mountains,
Be they on the fishes of the currents,
Be they on the examiners of the boughs,
Since these are the ones that can best bear it.

One third today,
Two thirds tomorrow,
And all thirds till doom
The day after that.[24]

This fine full gift of cursing, although here used to turn back the cursing of another, is a reminder that the Gaels had a long tradition of satirical abuse dating from the days of the druids, when it was said you could be cursed to death by their fluency and their venom. Clearly the gift of eloquent abuse continued into Christian times, with a token preliminary invocation of the Trinity or the saints at beginning or end of an otherwise pagan flow of vituperation.

Bad-mouthing

There were occasions too when a person in a close-knit community could be so "bad-mouthed" or unfairly gossiped about, that he or she would make a public petition to defend themselves against the gossip by going to a township *mod* or gathering and saying the following rune.

Petition against bad-mouthing

I will close my fist
Fitly around my stick,
'Tis to blot out bad-mouthing
That I am come within.

The three sons of King Cluanie,
And Manann son of King Lear,
And the young son of the King of the Green Vesture,
'Tis they will set me free this night.

Finn the Prince of the Fiann
Shall deliver me from the lie,
And brave Cool of the sharp blades
And Goll of the blows will shield me.

Brian the melodious will bless me,
And Briais of virtue will aid me,
And Columba the Cleric,
And Alexander, against venom.

The seven hosts of the Fiann
With their sharp blades will shield me,
And the young son of the King of Greece
Will take back the black slanders from me.

I will go down with Fite,
Brigid will raise up my head —
'Tis to take the face from slander
That I am come here.[25]

Una MacDonald of Iochdar in South Uist, who recited this
petition against malicious gossiping, as she remembered it,
said that the person suffering from bad-mouthing would stand
there with staff in hand and wit upon tongue, looking round
defiantly upon those present, and saying the rune in full
assurance that it would obtain a hearing and be effective in
stemming the black gossip. This too was a form of healing —
a very necessary healing of the emotional wounding that can
go on intentionally or unintentionally in small close-knit
communities.

In modern times this wounding still goes on in rural parts,
but sufferers usually have no resource but to ring the nearest
Samaritans, for the old community self-regulating sanctions and
ceremonies have gone. We are at the end of an era of poetic and

personal satire and counter-satire, cursing and counter-cursing, except for very occasional and partial survivals. For example, in a rural part of Ireland in 1991 two youths broke into an old woman's house and robbed her. But she was not as powerless as they thought, for so effective was the detailed and fluent curse she put upon them that they could not get any peace of mind till they went back to persuade her to lift the curse — and they were caught by the Gardai. The famous ready eloquence of the Gael can be both a wounding and a healing.

7. Woman of the fays

Origins of the fairy people

Roderick MacNeill, a famous story teller of Barra, explained the origins of the fairies like this:

> The proud angel fomented a rebellion among the angels of heaven, where he had been a leading light. He declared that he would go and found a kingdom of his own. When going out of heaven the proud angel brought prickly lightning and biting lightning out of the doorstep with his heels. Many angels followed him — so many that at last the Son cried out, "Father, Father, the place is being emptied!" Whereupon the Father ordered the gates of heaven and hell to be closed. This was instantly done; and those who were in were in, and those who were out were out; while the hosts who had left heaven and had not reached hell, flew into the holes of the earth like the stormy petrels. These are the fairy folk — ever since doomed to live under the ground, and only allowed to emerge when and where the King permits. They are never allowed abroad on Thursday, that being Columba's day, nor on Friday, that being the Son's day, nor on Saturday, that being Mary's day, nor on Sunday, that being the Lord's day ... On certain nights when their bowers are open and their lamps are lit, and the song and dance are moving merrily, the fairies may be heard singing lightheartedly:
>
> > Not of the seed of Adam are we,
> > And not Abraham is our father,

But of the seed of the Proud Angel,
Driven forth from heaven.[1]

A seventeenth century Scottish minister, Robert Kirk, was of
much the same opinion about the fairies, when he wrote in *The
Secret Commonwealth of Elves, Fauns and Fairies:*

> These *siths* or Fairies are said to be of middle Nature,
> betwixt Man and Angel, as were demons thought to be of
> old; of intelligent, studious Spirits, and light changeable
> Bodies (lyke those called Astral) somewhat of the Nature
> of a condensed Cloud, and best seen in Twilight ... Their
> Apparell and Speech are lyke that of the people and
> Country under which they live.

The Reverend Kirk, according to hearsay, was punished by the
fairies for publicizing their secrets in his writings, and for
walking over their knolls. To have anything to do with the fairy
world carries risk and uncertainty for humans. The fairies objec-
ted to the Reverend Kirk on the quite understandable grounds
that he was prying on them for his own advantage and to satisfy
the unearned curiosity of his readers (the sin of the media
throughout history). But other humans could get involved accidentally in fairy feasts and dancing inside the fairy knolls or on
the fairy circles (where the grass shows a brighter green on
pasture), and they too would suffer. When they escaped back to
their own world, they generally found that a hundred years had
passed in a night, and they themselves had aged accordingly.
Yet the fairy hospitality is irresistible:

> The slender woman of the green mantle and the yellow
> hair is wise of head and deft of hand. She can convert the
> white water of the rill into rich red wine, and the threads
> of the spider into a tartan plaid. From the stalk of the
> fairy reed she can bring the music of repose and peace,
> however active the brain and lithe the limb; and she can
> rouse to mirth and merriment, and to the dance, men and
> women, however gloomy their condition. From the bower
> in the green hillock could be heard the pipe and the song

and the voice of laughter as they sett and reeled in the
mazes of the dance. Sometimes a man seeing the wonder-
ful light and hearing the merry music, would be tempted
to go in and join them, but woe to him if he omitted to
leave a piece of iron at the door on entering, for the
cunning fairies would close the door and the man would
find no egress. There he would dance for years, but to
him the years were as one day — while his wife and
family mourned him as dead.[2]

But, added this Gaelic story teller, "faith is dead, and such
things do not happen now." Indeed, fairy stories are now largely
confined to children's books, and even there the intra-terrestrial
fairy folk are losing ground to the extra-terrestrials. But
although the telling of fairy stories is in decline, the interpreta-
tion of them goes on apace, for all over the world there are
variants of the same archetypal themes of good and evil; the
quest for a lost paradise which can only succeed by overcoming
difficulties and avoiding taboo-breaking; and transformations
which occur when ordinary conventions are set aside for pro-
founder truths. Encounters with the Otherworld of the fairies
involve heavy risks of loss of identity and security, and there is
no guarantee that personal transformation will be the kind one
wants, or that it will be reversible. A brush with the fairies may
only mean disappearing into a world of fantasy and losing all
touch with reality. It can be seen that there are parallels
between psychological states and fairy encounters, and some
therapists get their clients to explore their psychological
problems through the media of fairy stories. It may therefore be
of interest to see how in the Gaelic fairy world humans can
learn to get the better of the magical powers which threaten to
overwhelm them (though they may be helpful, too, of course, for
the Otherworld is essentially ambiguous).

Outwitting the fairies

Here is a typical exchange between a fairy woman and a mortal
woman which demonstrates the cosmic necessity for the weaker

to be able to outwit the stronger, for otherwise, if you give them
an inch they will take a mile.

> A fairy woman came to where a mortal woman was
> nursing a little child. She stood stubbornly, stiffly, starkly
> before the child, peering and staring at it straight in the
> face. At last she said:
> "Comely is your child, woman," says the fairy woman.
> "Comely is every lucky earthling," says the nurse.
> "Green is your child, woman," says the fairy woman.
> "Green is the grass, but it grows," says the nurse.
> "White of skin is your child," says the fairy woman.
> "White of skin is the snow of the peaks," says the
> nurse.
> "Pretty and golden are your child's curls," says the
> fairy woman.
> "Pretty and golden is the daisy of the plain," says the
> nurse.
> "Sharp and cutting is your tongue, woman," says the
> fairy woman.
> "It was never set to a grindstone," says the nurse.
> When the fairy woman saw that the mortal woman
> would not yield her an inch here or there, down nor up,
> she turned the back of her head to her and departed by
> the way she had come, and never did herself nor any of
> her people come again upon that ground.[3]

The same kind of outwitting was felt to be necessary in everyday
encounters, when for example strangers praised a person's
belongings or livestock in what was felt to be an intrusive or
overweening manner. You had to outdo such interfering cheek
by going one better than them in valuing your own possessions,
to forestall their possible malice or coveting. Prying strangers
are an invasion of personal space and have to be outsmarted, for
knowledge is to be given only to people who are ready for it and
can be trusted with it.

The hosts of the air

With the coming of Christianity there was great confusion over the ancient belief in the hosts of the air. Were these the fallen angels who had become the fairy people, or were they the spirits of the dead who could not find rest till they had completed whatever unfinished business they had left undone in their mortal lives? In pagan times it was believed that there were spirits in everything, everywhere, whether animate or inanimate, so the hosts of the air were the movements of these spirits about the world, for good or bad — they were part of the flow of the cosmos. Christian beliefs caused some attempt to square the old and new religion, but not much, as this account shows:

> The spirits fly about in great clouds, up and down the face of the world like starlings, and come back to the scenes of their earthly transgressions. No soul of them is without the clouds of earth, dimming the brightness of the works of God, nor can any win heaven till satisfaction is made for the sins of earth. In bad nights the hosts shelter themselves behind little russet docken stems and little yellow ragwort stalks. They fight battles in the air as men do on earth. They may be heard and seen on clear frosty nights, advancing and retreating, retreating and advancing, against one another ... They commanded men to follow them, and men obeyed, having no alternative. It was these men of earth who slew and maimed at the bidding of their spirit-masters, who in turn ill-treated them in a most pitiless manner. They would be rolling and dragging and trouncing them in mud and mire and pools ... There is less faith now and people see less, for seeing is of faith.[4]

Unexpected blows of fortune, or sudden disasters, were the bolts from the blue, that is, the fairy darts or arrows that were launched in malice by the hosts of the air or the fairies of the knoll. To protect yourself against such onslaughts it was wise to carry a bunch of the blessed plant, *am mothan,* pearlwort, or St

John's wort, under the armpit inside shirt or bodice. You would
be safe too if you had drunk the milk from a cow that had the
mothan growing in her pasture, for, as one lascivious fairy
woman said to another about the beautiful youth who had fallen
asleep on their knoll, "I cannot cast the arrow of desire at him
when the blessed milk of the innocent cow that ate the beloved
mothan is in his belly."

Not all encounters between fairies and humans were
malevolent, for young John MacCrimmon of the famous piping
family of Skye was one day practising in the Hollow of the
Pipers at Bororaig, when a fairy woman came out of the knoll
and made him the gift of a fairy chanter, saying:

> Your beauty and the music of your piping
> Have brought a fairy lover out to you,
> I put in your hand this silver chanter
> To be eternal melody under your fingers.

But the hosts of the air, like good and bad luck throughout
human history, were no respectors of worldly status or wealth
or youth; they could descend without warning and wreak havoc
on lives, as in this curious tale of the *King of France's Daughter:*

> The beautiful daughter of the King of France was taken
> up by the host and carried about in the air, over lands
> and seas, continents and islands, till they came to the
> little island of Heistamal, behind Creagorry, in Ben-
> becula, where they laid her down in such an injured state
> that she died from the hard treatment; not, however, till
> she had told about the lands to which she had been
> carried, and of the great hardships she had endured
> while travelling through space. The people of the island
> buried the princess where she had been found.[5]

The only good that could come of the hosts of the air, it seems,
was the strange stories you could tell about far-flung countries,
and that did not save you from meaningless exhaustion. Is there
a hint of Nostradamus-type prophecy here about the horrors of
modern flying?

Fairy lovers and unwanted babies

Young women who became pregnant, and who were unwilling or
unable to explain how it happened, were said to have had a fairy
lover. It was particularly likely to happen to them when herding
cows on lonely pastures on drowsy summer days, as in this story
told by an old lady in Uist:

A farmer's daughter was once herding her father's big
cattle and followers in Trosairigh in the upland of Corry
Corodale in Uist. The day was warm and sultry, and
what but a drowse of sleep and a heaviness of slumber fell
upon the girl. When she awoke the cattle were missing.
She had no news of the cattle, and the cattle had no news
of her. But as it drew towards evening the cattle came
home, sauntering at their own sweet leisure, and the girl
came home with a hasty step after them. She came, my
dear, Oh she came home, and neither herself nor others
knew where she had been — O Mary Mother, neither she
herself nor anybody else knew at all where she had been.
But three quarters after that the girl had a baby son.
The girl herself didn't know, nor did anybody else know,
who the father was ... But there was a fair green fairy
knoll in the upland of the Corry, full of fairies — oh, a
great troop of the fairy folk with their fine green mantles
and their brave handsome costumes. People suspected
one of these.
The girl was advised to go to an old man who was in
the townland and to seek advice and take counsel of him.
She did that, and the advice she got was this: she should
go and leave the baby close by the green mound where
the sleepers rested, and where the drowsiness and heaviness of sleep had come over her, and stay hidden, and
overlook and overhear to discover whatever she might see
and hear.[6]

The girl did as she was told, and saw a fairy man come out and
pet the baby, singing and soothing it with "mouth-tunes like

none that ear had ever heard before in the land of the living," in
these words:

> What, my pet, shall I do for you?
> What food and clothing give to you?
> I'm fearing you will get the hiccoughs,
> And you not on your mother's breast.
>
> Och, it's a sorry state I'm in —
> You have broken the cockle shells of my heart.
> Better to be in the land of the dead
> Than be helpless and you wailing.
>
> I had rather than all my plenty,
> I had rather than all my living,
> I had rather than your breast milk
> That you were beside your mother.
>
> I'll carry you home to the fairy bower,
> And you shall have food in plenty,
> Titbits and milk, butter and cheese,
> And the milkings of the cow folds.[7]

In most of these songs the fairy men reprove the mortal women
for abandoning their babies on the windswept hillside, and
leaving it to the fairies to save them. There is an echo here of
folk tales of all ages and places, where unwanted babies are left
to die in remote spots, unless fate intervenes and they are saved
by a passing shepherd, as in the case of Oedipus, or good fairy
(father or not).

Mor, my beloved

> I rose unready,
> I rose unwilling,
> I rose unready —
> Better for me not to rise!
> 'Twas my utter bereaving
> That brought me out.

The calf of my calf,
The calf of my calf,
The calf of my calf
Lies by a knoll-side,
Without fire,
Without comforting or sheltering.

The mist was on the hill,
The mist was on the hill,
The mist was on the hill
And on the scree,
When she came to meet me,
The bright-faced girl.

'Tis the milk-pale, brown-haired girl,
'Tis the milk-pale, brown-haired girl,
'Tis the milk-pale, brown-haired girl
Who had the baby to me —
But not tenderly
Has she nurtured it.

O Mor, my beloved,
O Mor, my beloved,
O Mor, my beloved,
Turn to your little son.
Cold is the place
You have left him in.

Cold is the spot,
Cold is the spot,
Cold is the spot
On the lip of the hollow.
Cold is my calf
By the side of a hillock.

O Mor, my beloved,
O Mor, my beloved,
O Mor, my beloved,
Turn to your little son,

And you will get from me
A string of speckled trout.

Cold is the night,
Cold is the night,
Cold is the night
Tonight for a tiny boy,
And him without clothing
By a knoll-side.

You would get wine,
You would get wine,
You would get wine
And everything you desire,
You would get from me
The trout at the lochside.

The calf of my love,
The calf of my love,
The calf of my love
Is by a knoll-side,
With never a fire,
Freezing, without shelter.

I would give you silk,
I would give you silk,
I would give you silk
And everything you desire,
O Mor, my beloved,
Turn to your little son.

I would kill the deer for you,
I would kill the deer for you,
I would kill the deer for you,
And everything you desire,
Save that I would not rise
With you in the morning.

> O Mor, my beloved,
> O Mor, my beloved,
> O Mor, my beloved,
> Turn to your little son.
> Cold is the place
> You have left him in.[8]

When a string of trout comes into the story, it usually means that the woman's fairy lover is the dreaded "water-horse," temporarily shape-shifted into a beautiful youth for the purposes of seduction. The only way you can tell is if, while you fondle his hair, you come across a few bits of waterweed clinging to his curls. But that may be too late, as in the story told by Janet Currie, *née* MacDonald, of Iochdar on Uist:

The daughter of a farmer in Ormacleit used to go out to Benmore to Coire Mhic Iain with fodder for the cattle. Every day the girl went out she found a string of trout beside the lochan, and she used to bring the string of trout home, and not a living soul knew who was leaving the trout or where they were coming from. One fine day a good-looking young fellow met the girl and he greeted her in soft fair-spoken words, and the girl answered the young man in gentle agreeable words. The young man had a string of fish in his hand and he told the girl to come and rub his hair for him and that she would have the string of fish. The youth sat down on a hillock and the girl sat beside him ... He put his head in her lap and he fell fast asleep. The girl was running her fingers through the youth's hair and what was she finding there but waterweeds. She realized that it was the water-horse she had to do with and her heart started with fear — she knew very well he was not a right-thinking man. She took her scissors from her pocket and cut the girdle of her coat and she left the coat under the head of the man who was sleeping and made off home at speed. [As usual the girl had a baby as a result of her meeting with the fairy lover.] The girl was bedridden for three years with the fright she had got. Then one summer's day she was

sunning herself on the knoll behind her father's house,
playing with the little children and the sunbeams, and
who should she see coming but the water-horse in the
shape of a man. Her heart leapt from her with fear and
she was dead.[9]

In many of these tales the unwanted baby abandoned on the
green hillside is saved by a kindly fairy man and taken off to the
Otherworld of feasting and music. In a few, however, there is a
more punitive moral ending, where the brothers of the un-
married mother go out in pursuit of her mystery lover and kill
him, and are in turn cursed by the girl for doing so. But sometimes she relents and removes the curse in a Christian turn to
the story, as in this dialogue between sister, brother and mother:

> *Brother:*
> I saw your dearest yesterday,
> And he was asking after you truly.
> *Sister:*
> How was my lover
> When he remembered me?
> *Brother:*
> I was hitting him to hell,
> To the north and to the south,
> With my bright blade and my axe,
> With my left hand and my right.
> *Sister:*
> If you have really killed my Oscar,
> Up with you and lave those hands,
> Be that the last leeching
> From which your body and bones will bleach.
>
> May there be no growth on your rushes,
> May there be no butter on your milk,
> Nor a month old child in your house
> To cheer its mother out of weariness.
> *Mother:*
> Be you split like the freshwater salmon
> Between your two breasts and your belly,

And may the poisonous serpent be
Beside you, and no saving from it.
Sister:
The wicked wish I made on my brother,
Be it not on him it stays after all,
But on the rugged brindled hills
And on two thirds of yonder glen.

Fairy vengeance

Fairy women who took mortal men as lovers had a different problem. Their men eventually left them and married ordinary human women, leaving the fairy women full of the pain and the envy and the desire for revenge that come with a lover's desertion. For "the fairy women are like the world women, cold and keen and cutting to her who has come between themselves and the heart of the son of man," said Mary MacMillan of Iochdar on Uist, as she told the tale of the fairy woman and the deer hunter.[10]

A hunter fell in love with a fairy woman in a remote glen, but eventually he left her and married a mortal woman, and she was filled with grief and pain and sorrow, but bided her time till the hunter's wife was about to give birth to her first child. The deer hunter met the fairy woman as he was on his way to bring the midwife, and she gave him a gossamer girdle to put round the loins of his wife "that would bring her back from death to life though the nine deaths were in her mouth." She put him under a sleep spell and sang her sorrows and her malice into his ear while he slept:

Fairy woman's lament for her human lover

'Tis poor work for a traveller
To linger and to dally,
'Tis bad doing for a wayfarer
To be sleeping on the cairns,
While the young wife of ringletted head

Is being wrapped in a shroud at home.
My advice is, lovely lad,
That you'd be better shunning me,
For there's lying in my hands
What will injure you without weapon,
What will leave your shirt
Both white and bleeding red!
'Tis time for me to be home
To the place of fairy meeting,
Where I'll find lovely men
And sweet-voiced caring women.

But you, Murdo MacIain,
Who was the heart of giving,
Who was the deer-hunter of the hinds
On the day of the bright sun!
On the high hill slopes you would go,
And bring down a whole herd of them,
Climbing the rough summits,
'Tis I would be after you!

There was a time when your promise
Was as the life of the sun to me,
And when your kiss was sweeter to me
Than to drink in the sun's rays.

The fairy woman finished her song and left the deer hunter sleeping on the hillside. When he awoke and started for home with the gossamer girdle, he remembered that the fairy woman had unwittingly named the plant that eases birth — the fairy flax. So he took that home too and placed it beneath his wife on the floor-bed where she was in her labour pains, and she was made whole. He put the fairy woman's gossamer girdle on a round pillar stone outside the door, and the pillar burst apart in fragments.

The moral of that story was, as Mary MacMillan put it:

"God be between us and the envy of every fairy woman and every world woman as long as we are in the worldly frame!"

Sisterhood between fairies and mortals

There was an element of sisterhood between fairy women and worldly women, in that all were adept at the skills of the house — the spinning and weaving, the quern grinding, the baking. Indeed the fairy women worked quickly and neatly and could clear a mountain of work in no time at all. But there was a price to pay, and the risk of not knowing what they would ask in return for help was enough to deter the woman of the house from summoning their aid. She took care to bless all her household gear to safeguard it from the fays and their mischief making. Occasionally good fairy women would voluntarily help to finish a bit of spinning or a web of cloth, during the hours of darkness, in which case it was important neither to ask them anything or to thank them, or they might never come back, for their ways were perverse and unpredictable, and they operated outside the Christian moral system.

Changeling children

Fairy women were always on the look-out for newborn human babies who had not been baptized, to carry off to their bowers. In their place they would leave an ugly ancient changeling, who was a voracious and greedy consumer of the household resources, but never grew any bigger, and caused the human mother heartache and exhaustion and shortage. If, when a child was born, the aid women failed to consecrate the baby to the Trinity by performing the lay baptism, the fairy women

> came down and lifted the child with them high on their shoulders, and out they went by way of the hen-hole, leaving an ancient changeling in the child's place. The child that was left was thriving neither by day nor by night, for all that he was eating and drinking, swallowing up and putting away, but if he was, what of that? — there was neither thriving nor growth on him, not an atom ... Every last woman who would come to the house

would say to the poor woman, "Is not your child small, goodwife?," "Is not your child weakly, goodwife?," "Is not your child green-looking, goodwife?," "Is not your child sallow, goodwife?," "Is not your child your sorrow, goodwife?" — the same dismal drone of disaster from every one of them, like the scream of the seagulls at the skate.[11]

The distracted mother of the changeling eventually went to get help from a wise old man in Benbecula, who gave her the following advice for getting back her own baby and getting rid of the changeling:

> Go to the strand and bring home a good supply of shellfish of every sort, and after parboiling the shellfish, scatter the shells on the bare flat of the floor around the hearthstone. Leave the changeling in the cradle and go out as if you were going to the well for a bucket of water. Don't go far, and keep an eye and an ear behind the door to see what you will see or hear. After that, you will go down to the shellfish strand, and place the changeling stretched out at the margin of the wave, and put a lullaby in his ear to send him to sleep. When the first wave of the rising tide strikes him the changeling will wail, but have nothing to do with him and don't let on at all, that you have seen a thing or heard a cheep. When you reach home you will find your own pretty youngster there in the cradle.

This is the lullaby that the woman sang over the changeling as he went to sleep on the margin of the wave:

Lullaby of the shellfish gathering

Sleep you by the wave's edge,
Sleep you, my dear one,
Sleep you by the wave's edge,
Till I finish the shellfish gathering.

Goats' milk I'd give you,
And sheep's milk I'd give you,
And mares' milk I'd give you,
Dear heart, if you were my own.

Ale and wort I'd give you,
And the bright barley of the plain,
And wine of the chalice I'd give you,
Dear heart, if you were my own.

The plucks and scrapings I'd give you,
And the lapwings' yellow eggs,
And the autumn carrot I'd give you,
Dear heart, if you were my own.

Maize pudding I'd give you,
Earthnut, fat, fine fare,
And the spring tansy I'd give you,
Dear heart, if you were my own.

Milk and feast fare I'd give you,
Cheese and crowdie and a dram,
And buttered kail I'd give you,
Dear heart, if you were my own.

Oatmeal porridge I'd give you,
And honey and foaming milk,
And goodish gruel I'd give you,
Dear heart, if you were my own.[12]

While the mother sang this lullaby the tide came up around the changeling and woke him again, and he howled and screamed, but she paid no attention, leaving it to the fairy women to come and claim their own, which they eventually did.

This story ends on a Christian note, in spite of the prevailing magic and counter-magic so far. The mother finds her own baby safe in his cradle when she goes back to the house, and gets a cleric to baptize the child, and after that "neither fairy nor elf nor pigmy sprite ever again came to trouble him."

The meaning of the fairy world

The fairy world is not restricted to our human sense of time and space. Great sweeps may be traversed in the twinkling of an eye, so a fairy host may cross continents in a night, or fly to Ireland and back on their ragwort stalks between dusk and dawn. Sometimes they allow a human to accompany them as a mysterious privilege which usually shatters the favoured one, and at other times they snatch up an unwilling traveller. Humans who accidentally or on purpose enter the fairy world lose ordinary time and space, and come out totally changed, aged in a world where all their family and friends have gone.

These transformations are seen by some modern analysts as metaphors for the spiritual quest. The fairy world is Magic Flute country, where you may be initiated into new mysteries which will reveal to you great truths, or you may be destroyed by your own frivolity and insincerity in the face of great truths. Part of it is luck, as well, since you may be saved in spite of yourself by good fairies, or the kindly fates — the Eumenides, as they are called in Greek myth. Much of it seems to be about the spiritual quest for the Cup of Wisdom, or Holy Grail, or Mary's Cup, as it is Christianized in the Gaelic story called "The Fairy Queen and the Cup of Mary":

> The maiden-queen of wisdom dwelt
> In the Beautiful Bower of the One Tree,
> Where she could see the world entire,
> And where no fool could look on her.

> Great grief was on the queen of fairy-land at seeing
> the want of wisdom in the daughters of men. And
> the fairy queen put her lips to the fairy flax, and every
> blade and plant, every frond and flower, and every
> bush and tree throughout the wide world breathed an
> invitation to the daughters of men to come to the
> knoll, and that she, the fairy queen, would give them
> wisdom.

> Much commotion followed this invitation, the whole

woman-world heaving and moving like the hill of the
ant, the byke of the wasp, or the hive of the bee. The
proud scorned, the foolish laughed, but the thoughtful
sighed. Some said that they were wiser than the fairy
queen herself, others that they had wisdom enough
already. But many dames and damsels came to the
knoll, some to see, some to be seen, and some to seek
wisdom. Presently the queen of fairy-land appeared,
holding in her hand the *copan Moire,* the Cup of Mary,
the blue-eyed limpet shell containing the wisdom of
wisdoms.

The lovely little queen was arrayed in all the beauteous irridescent hues of silver, emerald green and mother
of pearl.

> Loveliness shone around her like light,
> Her steps were the melodies of music.

With a grace of form and a charm of manner all her own
the fairy queen held up the *copan Moire* and invited all
the women of the world to come and partake of the
wisdom of wisdoms. A wave of derision moved over
maidens and matrons, like a wave of light over the green
and golden corn. But to all who sought wisdom in their
hearts the fairy queen gave of the Wisdom — to each
according to her faith and desire, till none was left. Many
came to the knoll too late and there was no wisdom left
for them.

That is why some women are wise and some are
otherwise.[13]

So it was that the term "child of the knoll" came to be used of a
woman who had good sense, a practical wisdom, a creative intelligence that was shrewd rather than, ironically, "airy-fairy." But
under the impact of Christianity the fairy women lost their
standing as the givers of wisdom to mortal women, and became
at best ambiguous and chancy helpers, and at worst baby snat-
chers and tricksters and unholy magicians who could foretell
deaths and disasters (for they lived in a non-linear time-warp).

They had to be placated with daily offerings, or combatted with Christian blessings.

The water-sprite, *loireag,* for instance, was always around when there was dairying or cloth-working going on, and would work mischief unless she was given little offerings of milk for herself, or unless the work was blessed by singing protective songs. The *bean-nighidh* or *nigheag na h-ath,* the washer woman of the ford, was another water spirit, whose special job was washing the shirts or shrouds of those about to die, on the banks of the stream or by the stepping stones of a ford. As she washed she sang the death dirge, lamenting the fate of the chosen souls, and it was highly dangerous to approach her or to try and speak with her. She sounds like a female version of Old Father Time with his scythe, but this female personification at any rate is expressing sorrow at the deaths and is preparing to enfold the chosen ones in her shrouds, rather than cutting them down as Old Father Time does, rather ruthlessly. The washer-woman is variously described as an Old Mother Time:

> she had the appearance of age, but if so, who could make out her age or period? Her face had become swarthy and her skin tanned like brambles at New Year, and she was as old as the mountain mist;

or as a more conventional "wee fairy" figure who could be caught as a curiosity, and tricked to pay fairies back for their trickery:

> a tiny wee figure of a woman down at the ford of the White River ... standing on a stone at the edge of the water, washing a shirt and singing a lament. The poor wee thing was so busy lustring the shirt and lamenting all those who were to perish that she was quite oblivious of anything around her.[14]

So the watcher was able to creep up on her and catch her.

The descent of pre-Christian divinities and spirits to tricksy fairies is illustrated again in the descriptions of the *gruagach,*

the spirit who presided over the cattle, and who could be seen
either as a fruitful and bountiful goddess or as a capricious
spiteful elf. All over the Highlands and Islands there were
"gruagach stones," often erratic boulders left by the ice age
freestanding in the glens, with hollows on their tops, into which
libations of milk were poured by the women after the evening
milking. Neglect of this ritual might lead to the death of one of
the animals, or breaking into the corn, or their stumbling in the
rough ground. A woman on the island of Heisgar gave this description of the cattle spirit:

> her rich golden hair falling about her like a mantle of
> shimmering gold, while with a slight swish of her wand
> she gracefully turned on her heel to admonish an unseen
> cow ... her mellow voice in snatches of eerie song as she
> moved among the grassy ruins of the old nunnery — all
> silent now of the holy orisons of gentle sisters.

The cattle spirit was held in ancient affection as another
account indicates, from a woman at West Bennan on the Isle of
Arran:

> The *gruagach* lived at East Bennan in a cave which is
> still called "cave of the *gruagach*" — and "cave of the
> monster." She herded the cattle of the township of
> Bennan, and no spring-loss, no death-loss, no mishap, no
> murrain, ever befell them, but they throve and fattened
> and increased right well.[15]

She awaited the cows of a morning with her golden hair stream-
ing on the breeze and her enchanting voice filling the air with
sweet melody — at least until in the early centuries of Christianity the Church tried to stamp out pagan offerings and the
Trinity was given to the Gaels as a form of protection against
their former pagan spirits like the *gruagach*. A curious story
about the departure of the much-loved *gruagach* of Bennan
expresses this struggle between old and new religions very
movingly and beautifully:

The people of Bennan were so pleased with the tender
care the *gruagach* took of their corn and cattle that they
resolved to give her a linen garment to clothe her body,
and down sandals to cover her feet. They placed these on
a knoll near the *gruagach* and watched from afar. But
instead of being grateful she was offended, and resented
their intrusion so much that she decided to leave the
district. She placed her left foot on Ben Bhuidhe in
Arran and her right foot on Ailsa Craig, making this
her stepping-stone to cross to the mainland of Scotland or
to Ireland. While the *gruagach* was in the act of moving
her left foot, a three-masted ship passed beneath, the
main mast of which struck her in the thigh and over-
turned her into the sea. The people of Bennan mourned
the *gruagach* long and loudly, and bewailed their own
officiousness.

So the Gaels retained an element of affection for the ancient
nature spirits who became the fairy people of the Otherworld
after the coming of Christianity, while at the same time including in their Christian runes of protection numerous references to the mischief and badness done by the fairies. It is not
at all as one modern academic would have us believe (Hutton,
in his *Pagan Religions of the Ancient British Isles*) when he
argues that:

> The folklore collections made in Celtic lands during
> the past two centuries show landscapes populated
> with horrific female spectres who prey upon
> humans or who are the harbingers of death ... They
> are all a vivid demonstration of the truth that
> deposed deities can very effectively be transformed
> into demons.

The Gaels in fact found a hospitable corner in their Christianity
for their dethroned pagan divinities, and kept their pagan folk-
ways going in their everyday healing practices, their work-
blessings around the house and homestead, and in their everyday invocations to their deities, which usually included pagan as

well as Christian models, as in these fine extracts from a wedding song.

The Wedding Song was a celebration of female virtues, in which, it becomes clear, the skill of the fairy woman and the courage of the pagan Queen Maeve the battler are extolled on a par with the virtue of the serene Brigid and the faith of the gentle Mary:

> Dark is yonder town,
> Dark are those therein,
> You are the brown swan,
> Going in among them.
>
> Their hearts are in your controlling,
> Their tongues are beneath your sole,
> Nor will they ever utter a word
> To give you any offence.
>
> A shade are you in the heat,
> A shelter are you in the cold,
> Eyes you are to the blind,
> A staff are you to the pilgrim,
> An island are you in the sea,
> A fortress are you on land,
> A well are you in the desert,
> Health are you to the ailing.
>
> Yours is the skill of the Fairy Woman,
> Yours is the virtue of Brigid the serene,
> Yours is the faith of Mary the gentle,
> Yours is the tact of the woman of Greece,
> Yours is the loveliness of Emer the Beauty,
> Yours is the tenderness of Darthula the delightful,
> Yours is the courage of Maeve the battler,
> Yours is the charm of the mouth of Melody.
>
> You are the joy of all joyous things,
> You are the light of the beam of the sun,
> You are the door of the chief of hospitality,

You are the surpassing star of guidance,
You are the step of the deer on the hill,
You are the step of the steed on the strath,
You are the shape of the swan of swimming,
You are the grace of all lovely graces.

The pure likeness of the Lord
Is in your face,
The loveliest likeness that
Was ever on this earth ...[16]

8. Woman of dying

In our modern western society, dying has generally shifted from home to hospital, though a great many old people bitterly regret leaving their own homes at the end of their lives. Partly for this reason and partly because we have not taken responsibility for creating dying ceremonies that are personal and have meaning for the way we live now, there is a dearth of domestic ceremonies for dying, and grieving is found embarrassing yet at the same time necessary, so professional "grief counselling" is a growing trend. Perhaps there is something to be learned from the Gaels, whose ways of dying were home-centred, rooted in community support, and marked by personal and community recognition of the dying one — in their living and their dying.

Ways of seeing the next world

Death is the journey home to a heaven, *flathanas,* which often harks back to the pre-Christian belief in the blessed isles lying out to the west where the setting sun dips down into the Atlantic waves. *Flathanas* is sometimes described as the Isle of the Noble, or the paradise of *Tir nan Og,* where men and women stay for ever young and lovely and heroic, enjoying the loving and feasting and conviviality (and in the case of male heroes, the fighting and hunting) in endless perfection, which they had experienced only imperfectly on earth.

The pagan Otherworld was a world of the living rather than a world of the dead, which specially gifted mortals might indeed visit during their earthly lives, and which was everyone's final home of the seasons. It lacked a hell until the monkish chroniclers Christianized the old stories of the Otherworld, so that by the time of St Brendan the Navigator there is an island of hell and an island of paradise among the three-times-fifty

Otherworld islands out in the land of the setting sun, and there is an island too for those awaiting the judgment day. In pre-Christian days the Blessed Isles included islands of women, probably a survival from the time when women withdrew at certain seasons to carry out their own spiritual ceremonies and celebrations in seclusion from men. The Celtic underworld which was confused with hell by Christian writers (*annwfn* in the Welsh *Mabinogi,* for example) is but one of multiple and diverse Otherworlds where there is feasting and living, fighting and loving according to one's heart's desire. The magic cauldron of Celtic mythology gives to each what each most longs for, so there are not the same general prescriptions of paradise and punishment that we get with the coming of Christian doctrines of heaven and hell.

The Christian death songs of the Gaels retain elements of this pagan way of seeing the next world, though many are perfectly orthodox visions of death as an escape from the sorrows of this world to sleep on the soothing breast of Mary Mother or in the arms of Jesus, as this first song shows:

Death song

You are going home this night to your home of winter,
To your home of autumn, of spring, of summer,
You are going home this night to your lasting home,
To your unending rest, to your lasting bed.

Sleep you, sleep, and away with your sorrow,
Sleep you, sleep, and away with your sorrow,
Sleep you, sleep, and away with your sorrow,
Sleep, you dear one, in the Rock of the fold.

Sleep this night on the breast of your Mother,
Sleep, you dear one, she herself soothing you,
Sleep you this night on Mary Mother's arm,
Sleep, you dear one, and she herself kissing you.

The big sleep of Jesus, the sleep beyond sleep of Jesus,
Sleep of Jesus' hurt, sleep of Jesus' grief,

The young sleep of Jesus, the healing sleep of Jesus,
The sleep of Jesus' kiss of peace and glory.

The sleep of the seven lights be yours, my dear one,
The sleep of the seven joys be yours, my dear one,
The sleep of the seven sleeps be yours, my dear one,
On the arm of the Jesus of blessings, the Christ
        of grace.

The shade of death lies on your face, my dear one,
But the Jesus of grace has His hand around you;
Nearing the Trinity say goodbye to your pains,
Christ is standing in front of you,
        and peace in his mind.

Sleep, O sleep, in the calm of all calm,
Sleep, O sleep, in the guidance of all guidance,
Sleep, O sleep, in the love of all loves,
Sleep, my dear one, in the Lord of Life,
Sleep, my dear one, in the God of life.[1]

The next song shows that marked characteristic of hospitality that is to be found everywhere in this Gaelic spirituality — and no less in the next world than in this world. Once across the dark river of dying, the soul escapes the pains and weariness of the body and is met by friendly emissaries of heaven. A guardian angel leads the soul upwards (marked by a twinkling light ascending the sky, or in the case of serious saintliness a thick column of light such as ascended heavenwards from the monastery on Iona when Columba died), and the Archangel Michael is there to offer a hospitable welcome in the friendly heavenly household.

Be every saint and sainted woman in heaven,
O God of the creatures and god of the goodness,
Be taking charge of you in every strait,
Every tide and turn you go.

Be each saint in heaven,
Each sainted woman in heaven,
Each angel in heaven
Stretching out their arms for you,
Smoothing the way for you,
When you go yonder
Over the river hard to face;
When you go yonder home
Across the river hard to face.

Be the Father reaching out for you
In his fragrant clasp of love,
When you go over the streams in spate
Of the black river of dying.[2]

The Gaels voiced fears of a painful dying, and a dying without opportunity to weigh up one's life and prepare for the final judgment where the life of a person would be measured in the balance of eternity, without excuses, without concealments. The wrath of God was imagined in different ways to fit an individual's particular weaknesses in life:

The black wrath of the God of life
Is upon the soul of anger as it goes;
The white wrath of the King of the stars
Is upon the soul of the dumb concealments.[3]

Yet the household of heaven would make many allowances for human frailty, the Gaels believed, just as in their own households they made allowances for weaknesses in everyday dealings of family and neighbours. So their views of purgatory were rather kinder than official church doctrine might approve. Purgatory, they said, was the "hell of the holy" where the good only stopped for a minute "to be fanned and fumed and freed of all earthly contaminations. They are fanned by the white wings of the bright angels of heaven ..."

Till they are whiter than the swan of the songs,
Till they are whiter than the seagull of the waves,

> Till they are whiter than the snow of the peaks,
> And whiter than the white love of the heroes.[4]

Children would have no problems either getting through purgatory, said the people of Barra:

> The lovable little infant
> Will go through the pains of Purgatory
> As the fearless dove
> Through the darkness of the skies.

Once in heaven the white ones remain friendly and concerned and ready to help the rest of us still on earth to get rid of our weaknesses and faults of doing or neglect of doing. The picture is of the family of heaven in the next world staying in touch with the earthly family in this world, of a companionable conversation that goes on and on between the world of time and the world of eternity.

This affectionate communication between heaven and earth made it very hard for the Gaels to support the "heaven or hell for all eternity" judgmental way of thinking. The ongoing conflict between the original message of Christ and the harsher orthodoxies of organized religion is beautifully captured in the story of Oran, one of Columba's monks on Iona in the sixth century. One day on Iona, Columba and Oran were arguing about the happiness of the good and the unhappiness of the bad who had passed on to the next world. Was heaven really totally good and hell without any saving grace whatsoever? Could the situation in the next world be so completely black and white, in the light of Christ's message of mercy? Oran said he would put the matter to the test in the very spot they stood. He would go down into the grave for three days and three nights to see what he could find out about the next world. Columba agreed and got the monks to dig a grave as deep as Oran was tall, and he went down into it and the earth was poured over him. At the end of three days and three nights Columba said to his monks that it would be fitting now to look on Oran and see what had become of him. They dug Oran up from the grave and these were his conclusions on the nature of the next world:

> Heaven is not as they state,
> Nor is Hell as they say,
> Nor are the good for ever happy,
> Nor the bad for ever in misery.[5]

When Columba heard these heretical but humane words from Oran, he shouted to the listening monks:

> Quick! Quick! Earth on Oran's eye,
> Before he starts more controversy,
> For fear of scandal to the faith,
> For fear of upset to his holy brothers.

Oran was buried once more, for good this time, and "Columba wept sorrowfully and heavily ..." for he was a holy man after all, as well as churchman. But though Columba had to temper his saintliness to the exigencies of institutional religion, the ordinary people could follow the way of Oran, convinced in their kindly hearts that the good God could not really mean any soul, however wicked, to be punished for all eternity, nor any heaven to be nothing but pure goodness.

Dying ceremonies

The Gaels hoped for "a good death," which would be "a pillow death" in their own home, where they would be surrounded by their near and dear, and hear the death blessing said over them by the "soul-friend," the *anam-chara*. They looked on good weather, a period of calm and brightness for the death and burial, as a good omen, for

> If there was peace on earth it was a sign that there was
> peace in heaven and a welcome for the one who had gone,
> and that the King of all creatures was at peace with him,
> and His own two mighty arms open to take the immortal
> soul to Himself ... If the day was wet or misty it was a
> sign that the King of the Elements was pouring wrath on
> the earth. If the day was black and dark and stormy it

showed that God the creator of all creatures, was pouring the black wrath of His Grief on the soul of him who had gone. If it was a day of snow this was a sign that the white wrath of God was upon the bruised soul that had gone over the black river of death.[6]

The death blessing intoned over the dying by the soul-friend was called "the soul-leading," "the soul-peace" or "the soul-soothing." Like the lay baptism it was usually done by a close friend rather than a cleric, and whoever performed this domestic sacrament was held in high regard afterwards by the family of the dying. This was not the only duty of the soul-friend in Celtic Christianity, for in the seventh century the Irish missionary saint Columbanus urged a private and personal counselling between lay people, women and men. The practice of mutual confession between soul-friends proved popular and successful, by contrast with the formidable public confession of faults in the face of the congregation which had happened in the early church and led to problems of evasion and self-dramatization at the expense of others. The soul-friend who led the death blessing was the one who knew the dying one intimately in life and had supported them through their earlier shifts and crises, as now at the end. Here is one example of a soul-leading for a dying woman:

> God, leave not this woman out of Your covenant,
> Nor the wrongs that she in her body committed,
> That she is not up to enumerating this night.
> The wrongs that she in her body committed,
> That she is not up to enumerating this night.
>
> Be her soul on Your own arm, O Christ,
> You King of the townships of heaven,
> And since Yours it was, O Christ, to buy the soul,
> At the time of the balancing of the beam,
> At the time of the calling in to judging,
> Be it now on Your own right hand,
> Oh, on Your own right hand.

And be the holy Michael, king of the angels,
Coming to meet the soul
And leading it home
To the Blessed Isles of the Son of God;
The holy Michael, high king of the angels,
Coming to meet the soul
And leading it home
To the Blessed Isles of the Son of God.[7]

Burial and mourning

Women's part in the death ceremonies seems a curious mixture of private and public roles, as if two traditions had uneasily coalesced, as probably happened when pagan and Christian beliefs met and had to find accommodation in a conservative community. Although minister or priest was needed to perform the Christian rites of the dying, according to Catholic or Protestant convictions about confession and repentance of sin and the promise of peace at the end, lay people played a significant part at the dying. Woman or man might be the soul-friend who led the soul-leading, and, until she was down-graded into a public weeper, the community mourning-woman had the significant task of reciting the family connections of the dead person, recalling his or her life and place in the township, and drawing attention to the wants of the bereft family in a way that might attract the practical charity of neighbours.

All the neighbour women shared in the communal grieving at funerals, for where there was community, there was a shared sense of loss and a personal identification with the sorrowing, as in this picture of a funeral procession setting out on the Isle of Lewis where the scene was described as

singularly impressive — the moaning of the sea, the mourning of the women, and the lament of the pipes over all as the body was carried to its home of winter, to its home of autumn, of spring and of summer [while the following hymn was sung]:

I am going home with you

I am going home with you
To your home! To your home!
I am going home with you
To your home of autumn, of spring and of summer.

I am going home with you,
You child of my love,
To your eternal bed,
To your long-lasting rest.

I am going home with you,
You child of my love,
To the dear Son of blessings,
To the Father kindly.[8]

The mourning-woman

Every district in the Highlands and Islands had its professional mourning-woman whose services to the community were recognized on a par with the aid-woman or midwife, for their roles were to ensure that the people came into the world and left it in as comfortable and fitting a fashion as personal attention could ensure.

It was the custom for the mourning-woman to follow the body to the burial ground. Her place was immediately behind the coffin, which she would strike and drum on from time to time in the rhythm of the procession, and utter eulogies on the dead. It was an opportunity to rehearse the genealogy of the family, too, however humble, for connections mattered and were of endless interest and a source of identity and security in the close-knit crofting townlands.

But the community mourning-woman was a disappearing figure even when Carmichael was collecting his lore at the end of the nineteenth century. Still he persuaded a Barra woman to resume the old practice once more, at the funeral of a young crofter-fisherman who had died leaving a wife and little children. This is how he described the scene:

His house was in *Lag nan Druisean,* the Hollow of the
Brambles, lying below Heaval, the highest hill in Barra.
The scene was remarkable; below and right before us on
its tidal rock stood the magnificent ruin of Ciosmal
Castle, the ancient residence of MacNeil of Barra, and
beyond this for twelve miles out to sea lay one behind
another the isles of the Atlantic, usually wild and foamy,
like lions at bay, this day peaceful and calm as lambs
tired of play. The *bean-tuirim,* the rehearsing or lamenting woman, was tall and handsome, though somewhat
gaunt and bony, with long features and long arms. At
first she was reluctant to sing, but by degrees she came
to use her magnificent voice to the full and the result was
striking in the extreme. She and I followed the body as it
was carried in simple fashion on three staves, with a man
at either end of each. The woman rehearsed the grief, the
bitter grief, of the winsome young widow, the cries, the
bitter cries, of the helpless young children, asking, plain-
tively asking, who would now bring them the corn from
the breird, the meal from the mill, the fish from the sea
and the birds from the rocks? Who indeed? No one now,
since he was laid low. She then rehearsed the sorrows of
the poor and the needy, the friendless and the aged
whom he had been wont to help. Who would help them
now? Who indeed? No one now, since he was laid low.[9]

Since, as Oran discovered, it is in the nature of things for good
and bad to be mixed up together, the mourning-woman might
abuse her role of trust in the community, and take advantage of
a funeral to improvize malicious verses against the deceased, if
he or she had been a personal enemy. On Tiree when Red
Donald was being taken to his burial, the mourning-woman
went up to the head of the funeral procession as usual, but the
elegy she sang was not the usual eulogy, as this verse indicates:

> Thou are gone, thou art gone!
> Thou art gone and hast remained not!
> We shall see thee no more,
> Black Evil Donald!

And as she sang each verse she squeezed the cat she had
concealed under her cloak, so that it would squeal and squall as
a derisory chorus. "The young were amused, but the older were
shocked."

Laments

Laments were sung over the dead, while the body lay at home
in the coffin, by the closest mourners. Many of these Gaelic
poems are marked by a concrete directness of feeling:

Death dirge

Who have you there upon the staves?
Who but my shoulder of support,
Who but my utter burning,
Who but my close comfort,
Who but my burning coal of loss,
Who but my dear one and my treasure,
Who but the sap of the sap of my heart.[10]

And here is a wife's death dirge on her loved husband, given in
its long-drawn out entirety for the cumulative effect of the slow
meditation on every memory of the departed that the wife
retains.

Mackintosh's lament

It is I am the woman of sorrow,
Wearing the cap of dolour,
Since all men have come to know
That on its crown is the favour.

It is I am in dire distress
Since in the earth they laid you;
Carry my blessing soberly
To the tower of heaven's stones.

It is I who am desolate
Since the start of the year;
But want no offers I
From son of earl or peer.

The day is bright and sunswept,
There is music on the lawns,
There is wine in largesse there —
But none will banish my gloom.

I will not go to wedding,
Never, nor feast nor fair.
Twas in the start of springtide
I received the arrow that pierced me.

Beloved was my sweetheart,
Beauteous branch of the clustering locks,
More fragrant than cinnamon
To me the breath of your mouth.

Dear to me was my lover,
Loveliest branch of the land,
As the garden of apples
Was your courting and laughter.

It is you who would never miss a step
When they played to you the dances,
And you would not bend the grass blade
Under the toe of your skimming shoe.

Hunter of the deer you,
Of the grilse on the waterfall,
Of the capercailzie on the bough,
White seabird slayer you.

My love and my joy,
Both early and late,
At feast and at fair,
'Tis your arrow pierced me.

It is I who was bubbling
With laughter, and bright-eyed,
It is I who am down now
Since my treasure lies under the sod.

The wines for the wedding
They went to your wake;
Ah King! was I tearful
While they drained the glasses.

'Tis I am the woman of tears
Every morning on rising,
Putting on the kerchief
Each feast day and Sabbath.

'Tis I am the girl of great grief
Who nobody would know now
Since the time a year ago
When I got your ring on me.

'Tis I am in sore sorrow,
In fits of weeping flow my eyes,
And I longing for the lovely youth,
Brave rider of fine horses.

I was a young girl, I was kertched,
I had my veiling, my mating;
Och now, look what happened
In the space of a single day!

I was wived, I was kertched,
I am a crying misery of a widow,
The cut of cuts is piercing me sorely,
And no plaster relieving me.

Dear is my sweetheart,
Loved while I live,
Loved here on earth
And in the court of the High King.

My love and my wanting are you,
My love and my playing harp are you,
My love are you and my promised one,
My only hope is in Paradise.

Young Ewen, you are fallen,
Young Ewen, you are fallen,
Young Ewen, you are fallen
In the gap of the wall.

The bald-faced horse threw you,
The bald-faced horse raised you,
The bald-faced horse threw you
By the site of the wall.

Oh! Had I been there,
Oh! had I been there,
Oh! had I been there,
I would have stopped you with my hand.

Young Ewen, you are fallen,
Young Ewen, you are fallen,
Young Ewen, you are fallen
In the gap of the wall.[11]

Compared with our modern practices of death and dying, death in the Gaelic culture was very visible and the grief of mourning was worked through in personal and public acts, with the help of neighbours and friends. When the body had lain in the house for two or three days, and people had come to pay their last respects, the funeral took place with ceremony, albeit simple and without much expense, for these were a poor people, materially speaking. There was the township's mourning-woman to recall the dead person's life and remind the community of the plight of the bereaved. There was the procession in which great numbers of family and neighbours joined. And afterwards, when it was all over and the body buried in consecrated ground, it was the practice to compose personal laments which movingly gave the dead an extension of life in song, and eased the grief of the composer.

Many laments were sung by women for their dead lovers and husbands, but there are other instances where it is the hospitality and kindly charity of the dead person to those in need that stimulated the lament. On Barra in the eighteenth century there was a brother and two sisters who were left orphaned and grew up together in great attachment and devotion. But the lad was carried off by a navy press gang and died after the struggle, or was killed. The sisters went literally mad with grief, wandering about the island from house to house, and going from one island to another, dependent on the charity of the people among whom they wandered. One man in particular was unfailingly good-hearted and considerate of their needs, and when he died they composed a number of laments to him. Here is one of them:

Lament for MacNeil of Sandray

Though you have died, love,
There was no call for you to die,
Och no! Och no!

Your little kebbocks of cheese
Had been set on the trestle.
Och no! Och no!

Your little kegs of butter
Had been smoothed by your hand.
Och no! Och no!

And your little chests of meal
Had been pressed by your foot.
Och no! Och no!

Where now will we go in our pleading
When we are starving on our rounds?
Och no! Och no!

Where shall we go to warm ourselves
And us chilled with the cold?
Och no! Och no!

Where shall we go for cover
And your hearth-fire dead?
Och no! Och no!

Who will we turn to and call on
Since your house, love, is cold?
Och no! Och no!

Though you have died, love,
It was never your way to be gloomy.
Och no! Och no!

There was call for you to stay, love,
And give crowdie to your folk.
Och no! Och no!

But, O Mary gentle, beloved,
Now be you kind to my love.
Och no! Och no![12]

9. Celtic spirituality for today

The Gaelic way of life depicted in the *Carmina Gadelica* was lived out in a close-knit community of place and family connections, which was hospitable and charitable to its own people, but suspicious (often with good reason) of the incoming stranger, who might bring material or spiritual destruction and loss on the beloved community. It was a world where women and men had their own powerful but separate spheres of activity. Our world by contrast has been steadily losing communities based on neighbourhood and extended family, and is in danger of bringing up a new generation who do not know the meaning of community, but see their world only in terms of interest groups and conflicts between Them and Us (any excuse will do — religion, race, colour of skin, class or language differences). Gender roles have become more flexible and interchangeable, but somehow most women who work outside the home find themselves bearing a double workload where the domestic burden wears them out and leaves little "quality time" for relating to partner and children at home. Domestic work has been de-skilled with convenient push-button technology in the kitchen, which is a brilliant time-saver for busy women but is hard to celebrate, as Gaelic women once celebrated baking the bread or churning the butter or making cakes for special family occasions.

What then has Celtic spirituality to offer us today, in our urban high-tech environments or in rural areas where agribusiness has taken over from small family farms, or where close knit village communities are often split by an influx of weekenders and commuters seeking some share in the fast disappearing rural idyll? Firstly, though, what is happening in the Gaelic heartlands themselves where the people over the centuries moulded and were moulded by that blend of Christian and pagan spirituality that is preserved in the *Carmina Gadelica?*

The Gaelic communities today

There is a revival of Gaelic language culture currently under way in the 1990s, after a century in the doldrums with communities eroded by economic hardship, emigration of the young people, and domination of the English language over Gaelic in education and public spheres. In 1975 the Western Isles Council, *Comhairle nan Eilean,* was created, and for the first time it became possible for a Gaelic-speaking area to shape its own education policies. All fifty-six primary schools in the Western Isles are now trying to give equal status to Gaelic and English, but preserving a language and culture through schooling is by no means straightforward. The schools have to cope with large numbers of monoglot English-speaking children (whether of Gaels or incomers) who need accelerated Gaelic lessons before they can take their place in ordinary classes without swamping the natural Gaelic speakers. And natural Gaelic speakers may take a somewhat satirical view of the ways of the Gaelic-speaking intelligentsia who are returning to the Islands now that there are increasing numbers of professional jobs for Gaelic speakers. One reflection of this trend is the quantity of Gaelic programmes on television and radio, including even the recent inauguration of Gaelic lessons by TV. Said one old crofter to me of this phenomenon:

> Oh, there's a lot of blether now about the Gaelic on the wireless and on the television. The wallet is open for the language. But what's the good of that when you can't hear a word of it in the pub or in any of these incomers' houses, or anywhere around, except where the old people are? Surely isn't it in the home that you need to keep the language ... The only story-telling and singing that's left is what they put on for the tourists in the summer months. It puts a bit of money into the pockets of the singers, surely, only half of them aren't even locals — they come in from places like Inverness.

There is another problem for traditional Gaelic speakers over this cultural revival. For many Gaels the Gaelic-speaking way of life is associated with poverty and low status and a religion they have given up, so some may opt for an English-speaking way of life for their children, even switching to English television when a Gaelic programme comes on, and making English the language of the home, because that is the language which gets you on in life. Teenage children too may turn away from Gaelic culture in the search for "style" and keeping up with their peer group. So however benign the public policy there remain palpable differences between the attitudes of your average rural Gael and the urban cultural nationalists who are doing so much to find official support and financial backing for the Gaelic cultural revival.

The role of the churches, Catholic and Protestant, in supporting the Gaelic Christian heritage, has been construed either positively or negatively, depending on who is making the judgment. The churches have been instrumental in keeping the Gaelic going in their services, but it gets harder as the proportion of English-speaking incomers goes up, and the number of summer visitors increases with the success of the tourist industry. A widely circulated joke has the minister announcing to his congregation at the end of an hour-long sermon in Gaelic, "Well, for the benefit of the many English friends with us today, I am now going to repeat my sermon in English." Some of the old people complain that the level of Gaelic young people acquire is not good enough for them to appreciate church Gaelic, so the ministers face a dilemma of losing the language heritage or losing even more of the young people.

Nonetheless, the churches retain and support a strong sense of their own close community, even if the corollary of that is that they are accused of being excluding in their securities of conviction, and of lacking ecumenical hospitality. Like Alexander Carmichael in his day, the Gaelic poet Derick Thomson has been a harsh critic of the austere brand of Presbyterianism which took root in the Western Isles in the nineteenth century. It shifted, he argues, the hospitable fires from the middle of the Gaelic home to become the fires of guilt burning in the individual sinner's breast. In his powerful poem *The Scarecrow*[1] he depicts the black-clad minister coming into the ceilidh house, scattering the playing cards onto the floor, and taking the goodness out of the singing and the story-telling through which the ordinary people expressed their heritage and got their every-day enjoyment. Their own old songs and stories gave way to new parables from the Bible and from Calvin's creed, which led to a rigid and repressive religion where the solitary conscience smouldered in uneasy guilt. And yet, as Thomson sees in an-other of his poems, *Although Calvin came,* the new creed could not stamp out the old love of the land and everything that was in it. So those who lost their land and were forced to emigrate suffered a double deprivation — the loss of their old songs and the loss of their beloved community of place.

Another of the modern Gaelic language poets, Donald Mac-Aulay, sees that you cannot change a people utterly by bringing the Calvinist creed among them. Once it became a sin to dance and sing love songs and tell old pagan wonder tales, the Gaels could still recreate something of their old spirit of fire and enthusiasm in the way they sang the Christian psalms under the new order. In *Gospel 1955* he describes a packed meeting house where the psalm singing and the praying cadences are so powerful that they seem to carry away the congregation on a tide that harks back to the ancient flow of Gaelic heroic poetry.

Tourism has of recent years provided a new reason and a new audience for putting on summer ceilidhs. For many visitors to the Highlands and Islands the most obvious manifestation of Gaelic culture is the many fine singers and instrumentalists who compose and perform with the traditional instruments and also with electric guitars and synthesizers. They draw on the tradi-tional musical lore (female soloists singing the old waulking songs that used to be sung around the trestle table at the finishing of the cloth making) but also experiment with contem-porary themes (sometimes in the fine satirical mode handed down from the old Gaelic tradition). There have been great strides beyond the "tartan and haggis" model which used to dominate in Highland pubs. Gaelic music has spread out from the local and national "mods" (Gaelic festivals) to a wider audience, thanks to the media.

In the early 1990s the government gave £3 million a year for three years to prime Gaelic TV and radio broadcasting, so that there are now regular Gaelic programmes of music and language classes and documentaries and even a soap opera, *Machair.* The independent Gaelic College of *Sabhal Mor Ostaig,* on Skye, offers diplomas in business and communications through Gaelic, as well as its traditional language and culture summer schools which have over the years attracted significant numbers of Canadians and Australians, the descendants of the emigrants who left these shores a century or more ago but handed down a residual longing to return some day.

It seems then that as more Gaelic medium jobs are created in teaching, tourism, the media and local government, the language and culture are in a hopeful position for moving forward into a creative synthesis of traditional and modern, which could be a real recreation of community. Enthusiastic incomers who have fled from the urban rat race in search of genuine community or spiritual values often take up the culture, and indeed adult Gaelic learners are a significant element in the cultural revival. But there are tensions between locals and incomers when the newcomers show "pushiness" and get on all the community committees and seem to be running things without regard for the reticent locals and their more easy-going ways of getting things done. There is too a tendency for outsiders to romanticize the Gaelic way of life, or to want to cling to a past version of it, when locals are working for a better quality of life in more secular though still hospitable and family-oriented communities. The Gaelic way of life moves on, retaining valued elements for locals and incomers, though it sometimes seems that the Celts in general have a problem with external images imposed upon them which have little to do with the truth of their own everyday experiences. But keeping true to your own experience is a central element in the Gaelic spiritual heritage, and needs to be at the heart of any authentic revival of Gaelic Christianity.

The Iona Community

A bridge between past and present

In the early centuries of Celtic Christianity there was a great
exodus of holy women and holy men who left their own communities to go on "the white pilgrimage" which would bring
their form of the faith all across the continent of Europe.
Columba, of a princely Ulster family, founded his monastery on
the tiny isle of Iona in the sixth century, as a base for going out
and converting the Picts. George MacLeod here refounded the
monastery in 1938 to create a spiritual centre that would try to
heal the divisions between religious life and everyday life,
between prayer and social action, between the holy and the
ordinary. Today the members of the Iona Community, lay and
ordained, male and female, from Scotland and many other
countries, work in the world, expressing their spirituality
through everyday teaching and caring, for "The great contribution of Jesus Christ to religion was that He did away with it,"
said George MacLeod. The Iona Community welcomes to its
centres on Iona and Mull people of every Christian denomina-
tion, people of all traditions and faiths, or of none. So besides
the hundred visitors staying every week in the Community itself
over the summer months, around one hundred thousand people
visit the island every year — tourists, New Age followers,
modern druids keen to celebrate the summer solstice where the
line between this world and the Otherworld is at its thinnest.
The Findhorn Foundation has a small retreat house on the
island, too, so every shade of the spectrum of spiritual seeking
is represented these days on Iona.

The present day Iona Community seeks to reshape Celtic
Christianity to make it relevant to our own problems and concerns, while remaining true to its roots in the early days of
Christianity. The emphasis is on wholeness — individual wholeness and the wholeness of creation. It follows that we cannot
separate out our spiritual selves from the everyday selves who
get up in the morning and go through each day's encounters at
home or at work, with family and friends and co-workers, for

better or for worse, with or without grace. Everything we do and think and say in our ordinary lives is a way of expressing (or failing to express) our solidarity with our own inner selves, with our community and with the rest of creation. "A time on Iona changes people ... The Iona Community does not believe that we are brought here to be changed into 'religious' people, but rather to be made more fully human ... In the words of the German martyr Dietrich Bonhoeffer, we believe that 'the Christian is not a religious person, but simply a human being'."[2]

The Iona Community Worship Book draws deeply on the Gaelic tradition for many of its prayers, starting with the belief that worship is not separate from the rest of our lives — "worship is all that we are and all that we do." It includes extracts from the *Carmina Gadelica* to express modern concern with healing, with ecological issues, and with peace between lovers, neighbours and nations. Those who visit the island during the summer may join the weekly pilgrimage every Wednesday, and go round the island on a walking meditation which lasts several hours and focuses on historical sites which are resonant with modern meaning: the ruins of the Nunnery speak of our neglected spiritual foremothers, for example, and the old marble quarry with its abandoned machinery reminds us of exploited natural resources (see Appendix for an outline of the Iona Pilgrimage).

Renewing community

The 1990s has brought realization of the perils of losing a sense of community. There is suddenly talk from politicians as well as theologians of the moral void in our society which can lead to reports of teenage girls battering an old woman to death, ten-year-old boys murdering a toddler, a thirteen-year-old raping his teacher on school premises, and, at the other end of the social scale, the huge financial frauds on pension funds by the Maxwell empire, and issues of public morality arising even at the highest levels of government. "If morality continues to become a mere matter of individual opinion," says the Archbishop of Canterbury, "our current society will continue to disintegrate." But

formal Christian institutions, whether Catholic or Protestant,
seem to the largely non-churchgoing public to be another part of
the establishment, giving their blessing to the system of the
marketplace, while asking for it to be more benign to the
excluded — often a contradiction in terms.

Only a renewed spirituality of base communities seems to
offer any grass-roots recovery from the moral void, and that
means, as in the Latin American base communities of liberation
theology, ordinary people working together in house churches or
other local networks, to revalue ordinary everyday lives and to
nurture relationships — at home, at work and in neighbourhood.
The best way of illustrating this is to meditate on three examples from our world today. The first comes from Cathy McCormack who lives in a Glasgow housing estate that is generally
rated near the top of the social deprivation scale. The second is
from Elsa Tamez, an ordinary countrywoman in Mexico, and the
third is an appraisal of a women's community development project in Sierra Leone. Far apart in time and place from the Gaelic
spirituality we have been considering so far, they yet weave
together the same vital threads of human wholeness. They are
rooted in the ordinary everyday tasks, committed to a valued
community, however poor and deprived, and in touch with a
vision larger than themselves.

Cathy McCormack lives in Easterhouse, a sprawling and
outwardly grim housing estate on the outskirts of Glasgow,
where social deprivation is endemic and crime is rife. But
even as her household reached rock bottom — her husband having been seven years out of work and the children growing up
in a place which, given choice, she would never choose, and
which offered little hope of good growth — she underwent a
spiritual renewal of a sort, which enabled her to make something good of the everyday things, and to energize herself and
others in her community who seemed to be at the bottom of the
heap:

> "I was so broken by it that I felt there was no point in
> living. I wanted to go to sleep and never wake up. Then
> one day something happened. It was a kind of awaken-
> ing; almost a spiritual experience." Cathy realized that

nothing was ever going to happen, that no one was going to rescue them. "I understood that my life is here in this place, and no fantasy of escape would help. This is where the wains must grow up and make their lives; here we must survive or perish together."[3]

From these roots in her everyday and ordinary life, Cathy McCormack contrived to nurture the green shoots of new growth. She became a committed woman in the cause of her own personal and community renewal by working with jobless young people and by exerting pressure on local authorities for improved housing. Her convictions are based on socialism rather than formal religion but it is possible to follow Christ's example without being a churchgoing Christian — Christ was a marginal person too, a man of the underclass offering no clever economic or social analysis, but a caring being scornful of the marketplace as the sole arbiter of human achievement.

Elsa Tamez in Mexico reminds us in this hymn for celebrating the Lord's supper that the sacraments can be given a concrete, personal significance when they are rooted in the local community's everyday circumstances, rather than formal and kept at a religious distance:

> Come,
> Let us celebrate the supper of the Lord.
> Let us make a big loaf of bread
> and let us bring abundant wine
> like at the wedding of Cana.
>
> Let the women not forget the salt.
> Let the men bring along the yeast.
>
> *All:* Let many guests come,
> the lame, the blind, the crippled, the poor.
> Come quickly.
> Let us follow the recipe of the Lord.
> All of us, let us knead the dough together
> with our hands.

All: Let us see with joy
How the bread rises.

Because today
we celebrate
the meeting with the Lord.
Today we renew our commitment
to the Kingdom.
All: Nobody will stay hungry.[4]

In the Gaelic townships there were (and still are in many places) powerful elements of hospitality and conviviality which can be significant in forming a strong sense of community and preventing alienated and aggressive acts. Women have always played a central role in this kind of community cohesion, and now in the third world especially this is being officially recognized by setting up networks of women in development. An FAO Project worker in Sierra Leone sums up the way that women's sociable networks play a practical part in the success of women farmers' groups:

Women are working all day long. Their duties are three-fold:
Economic — They manage the household economy and constitute labour force for economic activities like vegetable farming and soap making to earn income.
Domestic — They prepare food for the family and up keep the home.
Reproductive — They reproduce the family labour force, care for the children and bring them up ...

As a male extension worker, these are my experiences working with women farmers:
Women are quick to adopt innovation and therefore ready for a change ... It is quite easy and quicker to circulate extension messages amongst them ... because they have quite a lot of places to meet like at wells getting drinking water, laundering, cooking and working places, etc. I once met a farmer at a stream laundering

and telling her companion the present cost of chemical per tomato cup ...

It is easy to recover loans from women. My past experience with men always resulted in court cases. My conclusion is that a woman feels that it is a big slap on her face when she does not pay her loan and the amount is made known to her neighbours. They have no grudge against sharing knowledge with one another. I had a farmer who was successful with a new tomato variety. I organized a field day to her farm for other farmers to see and know what she had done. She took it as an incentive and had great joy and pride in explaining how she did her work ... They show the patience in marketing. They see to it that all they take into market brings in money ...[5]

Hospitality and conviviality

In these examples of women today working at the grass roots to renew their own communities spiritually and practically, there seems to me to be a continuing thread of personal warmth and cooperation which is very much in the spirit of the old Gaelic way of life. This suggests a possibility for us all of making our homes and our workplaces and our public commitments more hospitable and more convivial. To achieve this means reassessing the values we attach to traditional masculine and feminine roles, and working towards more public mothering and private fathering. Then we might heal the split between the aggressive amorality of public life and the ghetto-izing of nurturing and personal warmth to the domestic front, where women often "keep things going" with an instinctive need for emotional conviviality.

To practise public mothering and private fathering would mean that men as well as women truly value mothering qualities, so that nurturing and reciprocal attention find a bigger place in the world of work outside the home, and in the corridors of decision making, whether at local, national or international level. At present it often happens that women in the public world have little alternative but to mirror male roles rather than to add to and enrich the quality of public debate and action with different more convivial characteristics, which we are supposed to keep for private life. Yet there are signs that these very qualities of conviviality and emotional connectedness can help business success — but so far only in the world of small businesses where women are freer from the dead hand of institutional manners. A survey of small businesses[6] in Wales in 1990 reported that women had done better than men over the first fifteen years of enterprise allowances, because of their greater success on the relationship side, the interpersonal skills without which the product technology, however brilliant, cannot be successfully marketed. The connectedness, the interdependence that women appear to develop to a higher degree than men at present, can actually become a positive advantage to men and women engaged in small-scale businesses of the kind now advocated by green thinkers. It is not just that the enterprise provides concern and nurturing for its own staff (in the way of personal training and everyday attention to their personal needs and strengths). Convivial relations can enhance the attention given to the product and the customers, with attendant profit for the business as well as a more human workplace.

Celebrating the ordinary

Wherever we live and whatever we do, there are occasions in our everyday lives which are worth celebrating, where we can use or adapt Gaelic prayers and blessings to fit our own circumstances. The old house blessing, for example, can be used to celebrate house-moving or getting a home of your own at last:

> God bless the house
> From site to stay,
> From beam to wall,
> From end to end,
> From ridge to basement,
> From balk to rooftree,
> From founding to summit,
> Founding and summit.[7]

The house protection blessing can be added, in its original form or modified to suit the circumstances of a particular household:

> God bless the planet and all that's in it,
> God bless my partner and my children,
> God bless the eye that's in my head,
> And bless, O God, the handling of my hand;
> From the time I get up in the early morning
> Till the time I lie down late in bed.
> Bless my getting up in the early morning
> And my lying down late in bed.
>
> God hold safe the house and the household,
> God, safeguard the children of the motherhood,
> God, enfold the animals and their young ...[8]

Celebrating a new baby

Friends of mine have adapted the birth ceremonies given on pp. 73–79, gathering their friends around them on returning home from the hospital, and reciting either the *Aid-woman's Baptism* or the *Nine Waves of Grace*. The latter can be modified to include whatever qualities are wished upon the new baby to help and support him or her in their life journey, as here:

> A little wavelet for your happiness,
> A little wavelet for your kindness,
> A little wavelet for your generosity.
>
> A little wavelet for your strength,
> A little wavelet for your pluck,
> A little wavelet for your patience.
>
> A little wavelet for your means,
> A little wavelet for your health,
> A little wavelet for your true speech.
>
> Nine little palmfuls of grace for your wholeness
> In the name of ... [the Trinity, or local saints, or what-
> ever protectors are invoked for the child].[9]

All the friends present join in wishing the baby whatever good fortune or gifts they hold most valuable, each one holding the baby for a few minutes in their arms and speaking their good wishes, before passing him or her on to the next in the circle. In the Gaelic culture the baby would always be passed round the circle in a sunwise direction, to be in touch with the natural cycles of the creation, and to be reminded of the turning of the seasons and the phases of human life.

There is a further stage of well-wishing which can be recited as a safeguarding of the newborn from whatever ills and misfortunes friends present decide may need to be averted in this new vulnerable life that is beginning:

> The little drop of the Father, the little drop of the
> Son, the little drop of the Spirit, beloved child,
>
> To aid you, to protect you,
> To encircle you, to enfold you,
>
> To keep you from fear of violence,
> To keep you from dogs of war.
>
> To give you salve in sickness,
> To shield you from black miseries.
>
> To shelter you from the malice
> Of the dark ones within and without.

Celebrating community events

To show how the old blessings can be adapted while keeping the spirit, here is a ceremony used to bless a new community surgery in Portmadoc in the summer of 1991. It was devised by Dr Alison Hills as a celebration of the new purpose-built centre for her community medical practice. Everyone who came to the opening was able to join in the responses on the right-hand side of the service sheet, to keep the spirit of participation:

"I am among you as one who serves." (Luke 22.27)

Unless the Lord builds —
> They labour in vain who build it.

Unless the Lord protects the town —
> The watchmen guard in vain.

Our hope is found in Jesus Christ —
> God's stumbling block and cornerstone.

Let us bless this surgery in the name of the Holy Trinity,
in the manner of our forebears:

May God give blessing —
> To the surgery that is here.

May Jesus give blessing —
> To the surgery that is here.

May Spirit give blessing —
> To the surgery that is here.

May Mary give blessing —
> To the surgery that is here.

May Luke give blessing —
> To the surgery that is here.

May Dewi* give blessing —
> To the surgery that is here.

May Non* give blessing —
> To the surgery that is here.

May Gwenfrewi* give blessing —
> To the surgery that is here.

Both crest and frame —   Both stone and beam.

Both window and timber —   Both foot and head.

Both gate and door —   Both coming and going.

---

* Substitute local saints to fit a particular place, as here Welsh saints
of healing are invoked.

Both man and woman —   Both parent and child.

Both young and old —   Both wisdom and youth.

Both guest and host —   Both stranger and friend.

Peace on each place that lets in light —
                    Peace on each corner of the room.

Peace on each seat that offers rest —
                    Peace on each and everyone.

Peace of the Father, Peace of the Son —
                    Peace of the Spirit, Peace of the One.

Listen, I stand at the door and knock
If anyone hears my voice and opens the door,
I will come into that place.
I will eat with those who live and work there
And they shall eat with me.

Come, Lord Jesus, be our guest, stay with us for day is
ending.

Bring to this surgery your poverty —
                    For then we shall be rich.

Bring to this surgery your pain —
                    That sharing it we may share your joy.

Bring to this surgery your understanding —
                    That we may be freed to learn more of you.

Bring to this surgery all those who hurry behind you —
                    That we may meet you as the Saviour of all.

With friend, with stranger, with neighbour, with the well-
known ones, be you among us this night —
                    For the door of this surgery we open
                    and the doors of our hearts we leave ajar,

He brings the source of life —
                    He brings light to the world.

The light shines in the darkness —
> And the darkness can never put it out.

*The ceremony ends with all present asking for care on
their community:*

Where there is falseness —   Smother it with your truth.

Where there is coldness —   Kindle the flame of your love.

Where there is resentment —
> Bring trust and compassion.

Where there is anything we will not do for ourselves —
> Make us discontent till it is done.

And make us one community —   As you are one ...

Lord's Prayer

Conclusion

The Gaelic spiritual tradition is a vital source of practical and
moving ways of celebrating the ordinary events in our lives, to
make them special. It gives us a way of seeing the world which
is personal, concrete and direct, and discourages us from
shrugging things off with the evasive cry of: "It's nothing to do
with me — this pollution or child abuse or homelessness or cruel
gossip ..." To be rooted in a sense of community means interdependence, so it becomes harder to distance problems by
appealing to the remote reasoning of experts or by "leaving it to
them," whoever they may be.

Gaelic spirituality is about the ordinary everyday things that
we all share, and it encourages the voices of ordinary people
giving expression to their personal celebrations and griefs and
moments of hope and fear. Ideology is absent from this way of
seeing the world. Instead we are invited to give our direct personal attention to what is there in front of us — at home and at

work and in our communities, and to respond as human beings to the best of our ability. Neither mind on its own, nor emotion on its own, nor spirit on its own, is adequate to make that response. We need convivial thinking and a more hospitable feeling, which can only grow out of mindfulness to everyday experiences. It is through the everyday things that we learn how to move towards the wholly human — in ourselves, in other people, and in our communities.

In this spirit we ask whether the people we work and live with are any the better for our company, as in the old days in the Gaelic communities the Christmas mummers would appeal to the kindness and hospitality of the woman of the house in these words:

> We are come to the door
> To see if we are the better for our visit.[10]

Appendix

The Iona pilgrimage*

On Wednesdays, everyone on Iona is welcome to join the pilgrimage around the island, visiting places of historical and religious significance and reflecting on the journey of our lives and the life of the world.

The pilgrimage begins at the foot of St Martin's cross by the abbey, and this is the first stance:

> The high standing crosses of the Celtic Church suggest that worship often occurred out in the midst of the wide worship of earth, sea and sky. And the Celtic everlasting pattern of the weaving vine on the cross points to the intertwining of heaven and earth. As George MacLeod, founder of the Iona Community, says of Iona, "It is a very thin place. There is only a thin separation between spirit and matter." On our Iona pilgrimage we look for the spiritual at the heart of the physical world.
>
> > Bless to us, O God,
> > The earth beneath our feet,
> > Bless to us, O God,
> > The path whereon we go,
> > Bless to us, O God,
> > The people whom we meet ...

The next stance is the Augustinian Nunnery whose mute ruins have to speak for themselves, for the lives of the women living

* From pp.60–64 of the *Iona Community Worship Book,* Wild Goose Publications Glasgow, revised edition 1991.

and worshipping here have left no records. They are among our
neglected spiritual foremothers.

> The lack of historical attention to the Nunnery reflects
> the neglect of women in a society and church of male
> domination for centuries.
>
> Hand in hand with the subordination of women has
> often gone a neglect of the earth, and an abuse of the
> human body.
>
> One of the offerings of the ancient Celtic church to
> today is its greater balance between the feminine and
> masculine, as well as its celebration of the interweaving
> of matter and spirit, and its affirmation of the goodness
> of creation and the human body. St Brigid, for instance,
> in her leadership of double monasteries of men and
> women in the Celtic Church, stands for us as a model of
> equality between men and women ...

From the Nunnery the pilgrims make their way to the Marble
Quarry in the southeast of the island:

> Situated above some of the oldest stone in the world, the
> marble quarry reminds us of earth's evolution over hund-
> reds of millions of years, of our place in creation's history
> and our responsibility to care for the earth. The rusty
> metal scaffolding and heaps of abandoned stone in the
> quarry speak of a type of disrespect for the environment
> which we see on a much larger scale elsewhere in the
> world. In the marble quarry we reflect confessionally on
> the situations in our world where natural resources have
> been exploited, and where human lives have been broken
> and left in a heap all in the pursuit of wealth and power,
> and here we give thanks for the goodness of creation.

> > O Christ, there is no plant in the ground
> > But it is full of your virtue.
> > There is no form on the strand
> > But it is full of your blessing.
> > There is no life in the sea,

> There is no creature in the ocean,
> There is nothing in the heavens
> But proclaims your goodness.
> There is no bird on the wing,
> There is no star in the sky,
> There is nothing beneath the sun
> But proclaims your goodness ...

From the quarry the pilgrims walk to the bay at the southern point of the island where Columba landed from Ireland in the year 563.

> Having clambered up the beach with their leather-bound boat, known as a coracle, legend has it that Columba and his twelve monks climbed the hill to the west of the bay to confirm that Ireland, their beloved home country, could not be seen. "The Hill of Turning the Back on Ireland" became a landmark for them as they moved forward in mission. They established their monastic centre on the east side of the island around the present day site of the Abbey, and from there conducted a mission to the Picts in the north, to the Anglo-Saxons in Northumbria, and throughout Europe, reaching as far east as western Russia. St Columba's Bay is a place of leaving behind the past and of new beginnings in pilgrimage and mission.

> And now, may kindly Columba guide you
> To be an isle in the sea,
> To be a hill on the shore,
> To be a star in the night,
> To be a staff for the weak ...

The midway point on the pilgrimage is the sandy grassland on the west side of Iona, the *machair,* which was once the corn-growing land for the monastery bread, and is now common grazings for the remaining crofters on the island.

> So the *machair* is like a parable of sharing, of cooperation as opposed to competition. Here we share our lunch

together and give thanks, remembering that we are called
to share the gifts of God with one another and with the
poor of the world.

Each thing we have received,
From you it came, O God.
Each thing for which we hope,
From your love it will be given.
Kindle in our hearts within
A flame of love for our neighbours,
To our foes, to our friends, to our loved ones all,
From the lowliest thing that lives,
To the name that is highest of all ...

Continuing the circuit to the north of the island the pilgrims
arrive at a ring of stones where tradition has it that Columba's
beehive oratory once stood, his place of silent retreat.

Times of solitude and silence undergird the busyness and
demands of living interwoven with community. As well as
hearing the word of God through the scriptures, through
creation and through one another, we can experience the
word of God deep within us at the very heart of being.

Deep peace of the running wave to you,
Deep peace of the flowing air to you,
Deep peace of the quiet earth to you,
Deep peace of the shining stars to you,
Deep peace of the Son of Peace to you ...

From this Hermit's Cell the pilgrim route now ascends to
the highest point on the island, Dun I (the old name for
Iona was Hy or I), which opens out new vistas — often of
squalls racing in from the Atlantic to blind Iona in mist
and drizzle, but sometimes you can see long distance
views across to the mountains of Mull and Skye, and
Jura with its twin paps.
In the biblical tradition, mountains or hills have been
understood as places of new vision and transfiguration.
Also in the Bible the sea is portrayed as a place of risk,
which can suddenly and unpredictably blow into storm. If

Iona is like a hilltop experience of new perspective then often the places that we return to are more like the dangerous seas. On Dun I, we begin to refocus on those places of struggle in our world that we belong to and are aware of, and we offer a prayer for peace.

Peace between nations,
Peace between neighbours,
Peace between lovers,
In love of the God of life.
Peace between person and person,
Peace between wife and husband,
Peace between parent and child,
The peace of Christ above all peace.
Bless O Christ our faces,
Let our faces bless everything,
Bless O Christ our eyes,
Let our eyes bless all they see ...

Sources

The primary sources for this book have been the major collection of blessings and lore made by Alexander Carmichael in the Highlands and Islands of Scotland in the second half of the nineteenth century.

Originally published in a bilingual edition (6 vols) by Oliver & Boyd (and subsequently, Scottish Academic Press) between 1900 and 1961, the *Carmina Gadelica* is now available as a paperback in one volume (English language only), published by Floris Books, Edinburgh in 1992 (reissued and revised with full cross-referencing in 1994). For the convenience of readers who want to trace my extracts from the *Carmina Gadelica*, I have provided references to the Floris Books paperback edition, though in some cases my wording varies, because I have consulted a number of modern anthologies, and have sometimes modified Carmichael's wording to modernize his English or to stay as close as possible to the original Gaelic.

The references are to page numbers in the one volume paperback edition of *Carmina Gadelica* (Floris Books, 1992, reissued 1994), except in a few instances where I have referred back to the original bilingual edition (OE) where Carmichael's extensive Gaelic glossary or his Gaelic/English notes are found in Volumes 2 and 6.

Introduction
1 Catherine MacPhee p.632
2 Peggy MacCormack p.632
3 Mary Mackintosh p.282
4 Power of raven be thine p.267
5 Carmichael p.24
6 North Uist woman healer p.644
7 Roderick MacLeod p.656
8 Carmichael p.30

Chapter 1. Woman of the house
1 Blessing of the kindling p.93
2 Blessing the night fire (1) p.95
3 Blessing the night fire (2) p.297 (variant)
4 Sleep consecration p.56

Chapter 2. Woman of loving

19 St Brigid's charm p.134
20 The figwort is a blessed plant p.608
21 I will pluck the figwort p.149
22 Holy well for childlessness p.379
23 You will sprinkle the water p.643
24 I make to you, my dearest p.385
25 Petition against bad mouthing p.373

Chapter 7. Woman of the fays
 1 Origins of the fairies, OE, Vol II, pp.352f
 2 Slender woman of the green mantle, OE, Vol II, p.356
 3 A fairy woman came p.513
 4 The spirits fly about in great clouds, OE, Vol II, p.357
 5 The King of France's daughter, OE, Vol II, p.358
 6 A farmer's daughter p.664
 7 What my pet shall I do for you? p.484
 8 Mor, my beloved p.485
 9 Janet Currie p.665
10 The hunter and fairy woman p.483
11 The fairy changeling pp.517–22
12 Lullaby of the shellfish gathering p.521
13 Cup of Mary — wisdom of women, OE, Vol II, pp.255f
14 Washerwoman by the ford p.524
15 Gruagach/cattle spirit, OE, Vol II, pp.306f
16 Dark is yonder town p.37

Chapter 8. Woman of dying
 1 Death song p.312
 2 Be every saint and sainted woman ... OE, Vol III, p.203
 3 The black wrath p.309
 4 Till they are whiter p.634
 5 Heaven is not as they state, OE, Vol II, pp.315f
 6 If there was peace on earth p.634
 7 God, leave not this woman p.67
 8 I am going home with you p.311
 9 His house was in Lag nan Druisean p.551
10 Death dirge p.551
11 Mackintosh's lament p.553
12 Lament for MacNeil of Sandray p.552

Chapter 9. Celtic spirituality for today

1 "The Scarecrow," in *Nua Bhardachd Ghaidhlig: Modern Scottish Gaelic Poems,* p.164, Canongate, Edinburgh 1987; "Gospel 1955," ibid., p.192.

2 From *Iona Community Worship Book,* p.8

3 Cathy McCormack, in Jeremy Seabrook, *The myth of the market,* Green Books, Hartland, Devon 1990, p.102f.

4 Elsa Tamez, in *Women's Prayer Services,* (N. American ed), p.20. Twenty-third Publications, Mystic, Conn. USA 1987.

5 Sierra Leone women farmers' networks, in *Women's Link,* IV, Oct 1991, p.33, Freetown, Sierra Leone.

6 Women and small businesses, in *Cambrian News* Jan 1990, Aberystwyth, Wales.

7 God bless the house p.63

8 House protection p.63

9 Birth ceremonies pp.191–96

10 We are come to the door p.78

Suggestions for further reading

Anthologies from the Carmina Gadelica

Bittleston, Adam, *The Sun Dances: Prayers and Blessings from the Gaelic,* Floris Books, Edinburgh 1988; reprint 1993.

Waal, Esther de, *The Celtic Vision,* Darton, Longman & Todd, London 1988.

Jones, Michael, *New Moon of the Seasons,* Floris Books, Edinburgh 1986, reprint 1992.

McLean, G.R.D. *Poems of the Western Highlands,* SPCK, London 1961.

Celtic Christianity

Allchin, A.M., *Praise above all,* University of Wales Press, Cardiff 1991.

Bamford, Christopher and William Parker Marsh (eds.), *Celtic Christianity, ecology and holiness,* Floris Books, Edinburgh 1986, reprint 1992.

Waal, Esther de, *A World made Whole,* Harper Collins, London 1991.

Mackey (ed.), James P., *An Introduction to Celtic Christianity,* T & T Clark, Edinburgh 1989.

Matthews, Caitlín, *The Celtic Tradition,* Element, Shaftesbury 1989.

Thomas, Patrick, *The Opened Door, a Celtic Spirituality,* Silyn Publications, Brechfa, Dyfed 1990.

——, *A Candle in the Darkness,* Gomer Press, Llandysul 1993.

Toulson, Shirley, *The Celtic Alternative: the Christianity we lost,* Century, London 1987.

Celtic Saints

Floris Books, Edinburgh, publish short lives of saints from medieval or ancient sources, with introductions, in individual pocket books (1992): *St Patrick; St Bride; St Columba; St Brendan.*

St Columba and Iona

Adamnan, *Life of St Columba, edited by William Reeves.* Reprint by
    Llanerch Enterprises, Lampeter 1988.
Finlay, Ian, *Columba,* Gollancz, London 1979.
Iona Community Worship Book, (revised ed), Wild Goose Publications,
    Glasgow 1991. (The Worship Book incorporates some of the *Carmina
    Gadelica* in their original words, or modified for modern people.)

The Celts from pagan to Christian times

For understanding the pagan survivals in Christian times in the Celtic
lands, Miranda Green's *The Gods of the Celts,* Alan Sutton, Gloucester
1986, is very illuminating.

For a sceptical view of pagan survivals and neo-pagan revivals in
our own day, consult J. Hutton's *Pagan religions in the ancient British
Isles,* Blackwell, Oxford 1991, which is strongly dismissive of "pseudo-
Celticism."

Two old classics still worth reading are Nora Chadwick's *The Celts,*
Penguin, London 1976; and Joseph Raftery's *The Celts,* Mercier Press,
Dublin 1976 (Thomas Davis Lectures).

For a scholarly and yet "coffee table" extravaganza on the Celtic
pagan and Christian heritage, there is the book of the great *Celti*
exhibition in Italy in 1991 — Sabatino Moscato (comp), *The Celts,*
Thames & Hudson, London, 1991.

The Gaelic culture today

Chapman, Malcolm, *The Celts: the construction of a myth,* Macmillan,
    London 1992.
Crofters' Commission, *Annual Reports.*
Gillies, W. (ed), *Gaelic and Scotland,* Edinburgh University Press,
    Edinburgh 1989.
MacKinnon, Kenneth, *Gaelic, a Past and Future Prospect,* Saltire
    Society, Edinburgh 1991.
Stewart, Katherine, *Crofts and Crofting,* Mercat Press,
    Edinburgh 1980.

The best way of finding out about the Gaelic culture now is, as always
in the Celtic lands, to talk to people who live there, and to read the
community newspapers. The *Stornoway Gazette,* for example, gives an
everyday view of the ongoing impact of incomers and EC grants and
tourists and "Wee Frees" on the Western Isles today.